Salesforce Essentials for Administrators

Discover the administration fundamentals and challenges of Salesforce CRM

Mohith Shrivastava

[PACKT] enterprise
PUBLISHING   professional expertise distilled

BIRMINGHAM - MUMBAI

Salesforce Essentials for Administrators

First published: October 2014

Production reference: 1031014

Published by Packt Publishing Ltd.
Livery Place
35 Livery Street
Birmingham B3 2PB, UK.

ISBN 978-1-78439-807-1

www.packtpub.com

Credits

Author
Mohith Shrivastava

Reviewers
Chetan S. Bhelonde
Edwin Hendrick
Bhawani Shankar Sharma

Commissioning Editor
Kunal Parikh

Acquisition Editor
Sonali Vernekar

Content Development Editor
Shali Sasidharan

Technical Editor
Taabish Khan

Copy Editors
Karuna Narayanan
Alfida Paiva
Adithi Shetty

Project Coordinator
Neha Bhatnagar

Proofreaders
Maria Gould
Ameesha Green
Paul Hindle
Bernadette Watkins

Indexers
Hemangini Bari
Mariammal Chettiyar

Production Coordinators
Manu Joseph
Komal Ramchandani
Shantanu N. Zagade

Cover Work
Manu Joseph

About the Author

Mohith Shrivastava has been working with Salesforce and Force.com since 2011 after he graduated from The National Institute of Engineering, Mysore. He holds Advanced Developer, Advanced Administrator, Sales Cloud Consultant, and Service Cloud Consultant certifications. He has been actively contributing at `http://salesforce.stackexchange.com`. He is a micro blogger at `http://cloudyworlds.blogspot.com`. He started his career with Deloitte and is currently working for one of the Big Four consulting firms. His career interest lies in management consulting. He loves coding on the SFDC platform and is skilled in Apex and Visualforce. He was recently part of a team that won the Salesforce Summer of Hacks hackathon contest organized worldwide.

Mohith was a technical reviewer for *Developing Applications with Salesforce Chatter*, *Packt Publishing*. In his free time, he loves watching cricket and movies, hanging out with friends, and exploring web technologies.

I would like to thank my parents. I would like to dedicate this work to my mom and dad for their awesome support and encouragement, and for being my source of inspiration. I would also like to thank all the technical reviewers for helping me get better content. It's been an awesome time working on this after my office hours.

About the Reviewers

Chetan S. Bhelonde has more than six years of experience in software quality assurance. He has worked in different domains such as cloud and PLM, and platforms such as Salesforce and CATIA. He has had good exposure to scripting languages such as Python and VBScript.

Edwin Hendrick currently holds the position of Managing Consultant at Capgemini in The Netherlands. In this position, he focuses on designing and delivering packaged-based Salesforce CRM applications.

Edwin has ample experience with Salesforce.com and is fully certified. Among his areas of expertise are enterprise marketing and business intelligence. Over the last couple of years, he has been responsible for implementing CRM applications in an international setting. Currently, he plays a leading role in developing the Salesforce.com capabilities at Capgemini.

Edwin has completed his BSc in Marketing and his MSc in Business Administration from Rotterdam School of Management, Erasmus University.

Bhawani Shankar Sharma holds Developer, Advanced Developer, Administrator, Sales Cloud Consultant, and Service Cloud Consultant certifications from Salesforce.com. His passion is cracking Salesforce certifications and solving developers' questions in the developer community. He is an active blogger and runs `http://simplyforce.blogspot.in/`. He is easily reachable in the developer community, LinkedIn, Twitter, and so on. His personal e-mail address is `bhawani.sh.sharma@gmail.com`.

Bhawani has worked with many big companies and helped them increase their ROI. He is mostly focused on solutioning, application architecture, project management, and quality.

He has also reviewed *Salesforce CRM: The Definitive Admin Handbook*, *Packt Publishing*, which is highly appreciated globally.

Bhawani is married and has a boy named Aadi Sharma. He loves spending time with Aadi whenever he is free. His wife, Tanuja Sharma, has worked with Reliance for five years. She is now a housewife and takes care of Aadi whenever Bhawani is playing with technology.

www.PacktPub.com

Support files, eBooks, discount offers, and more

You might want to visit www.PacktPub.com for support files and downloads related to your book.

Did you know that Packt offers eBook versions of every book published, with PDF and ePub files available? You can upgrade to the eBook version at www.PacktPub.com and as a print book customer, you are entitled to a discount on the eBook copy. Get in touch with us at service@packtpub.com for more details.

At www.PacktPub.com, you can also read a collection of free technical articles, sign up for a range of free newsletters and receive exclusive discounts and offers on Packt books and eBooks.

http://PacktLib.PacktPub.com

Do you need instant solutions to your IT questions? PacktLib is Packt's online digital book library. Here, you can access, read and search across Packt's entire library of books.

Why subscribe?

- Fully searchable across every book published by Packt
- Copy and paste, print and bookmark content
- On demand and accessible via web browser

Free access for Packt account holders

If you have an account with Packt at www.PacktPub.com, you can use this to access PacktLib today and view nine entirely free books. Simply use your login credentials for immediate access.

Instant updates on new Packt books

Get notified! Find out when new books are published by following @PacktEnterprise on Twitter, or the *Packt Enterprise* Facebook page.

Table of Contents

Preface

Salesforce as a CRM and as a platform is growing rapidly, and the demand for good Salesforce administrators and developers is also increasing rapidly. The developers or administrators who enter this world often feel the need for a write-up, which will cover the basic concepts with illustrations. This book is an attempt to fill this need. To make the concepts clear, this book focuses on screenshots followed by their explanations. The prerequisite to understanding this book is a basic knowledge of Salesforce as a CRM. This book will cover concepts such as profile management, security management, advanced validations, advanced formula fields, approval process configuration, user adoption improvements through reports and dashboards, and basic sales and service cloud features provided by the Salesforce CRM.

What this book covers

Chapter 1, User Management and User Profiling, discusses the process of creating users in Salesforce and how licensing is managed. This chapter will discuss delegated administration in detail. In profile management, we will discuss how to manage profiles, field accessibility, various system permissions, the need for permission sets, mobile configuration, object permissions, the Apex class and Visualforce page access, and the Salesforce A application for the administrator.

Chapter 2, Configuring Salesforce, discusses the configuration components that cover data modeling, validations, record types, page layout configurations, workflows, approval process configurations, formula fields, and e-mail templates.

Chapter 3, Reports and Dashboards, explains the various types of reports and dashboards. It discusses analytic snapshots and the usage of the PARENTGROUPVAL and PREVGROUPVAL summary functions.

Chapter 4, Record-level Access, Security, and Audit Features, explains OWD, the sharing settings, manual sharing, role hierarchy, and audit features provided by the Salesforce platform.

Chapter 5, Session Management, Data Loader, and Data Loading Best Practices, focuses on the basic data-loading concepts using data loader, session management, and password-protection policies.

Chapter 6, Troubleshooting Common Problems, consists of common real-time business problems and the best practices and techniques to solve them using the components provided by the Salesforce CRM.

Chapter 7, An Overview of Sales and Service Cloud, discusses the sales cloud features in brief, which includes territory management and forecasting. It also discusses service cloud features such as entitlement management, knowledge management, and content management. This chapter ends with a discussion on Salesforce as a maturity model.

What you need for this book

This book requires no software. The reader needs to sign up for the developer edition of Salesforce and needs to work with the examples provided in this book to gain greater insights into the concepts discussed.

Who this book is for

Salesforce Essentials for Administrators is targeted for all professionals who have just started with the Salesforce CRM or Salesforce platform, and want to explore the basics in a very short time span. This book will help individuals prepare for the Salesforce Developer certification as well as for the Salesforce Administrator certification.

Conventions

In this book, you will find a number of styles of text that distinguish between different kinds of information. Here are some examples of these styles and an explanation of their meaning.

Code words in text, database table names, folder names, filenames, file extensions, pathnames, dummy URLs, user input, and Twitter handles are shown as follows: "You can use the PREVGROUPVAL function to calculate values relative to a peer grouping."

A block of code is set as follows:

```
IF($User.City = "Napa", 0.0750,
 IF($User.City = "Paso Robles", 0.0725,
  IF($User.City = "Sutter Creek", 0.0725,
   IF($User.City = "Los Olivos", 0.0750,
    IF($User.City = "Livermore", 0.0875, null
    )
   )
  )
 )
)
```

New terms and **important words** are shown in bold. Words that you see on the screen, in menus or dialog boxes for example, appear in the text like this: "For example, select **Leads** to view leads."

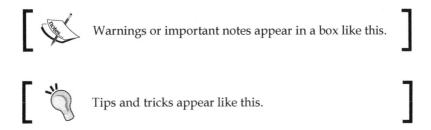

Warnings or important notes appear in a box like this.

Tips and tricks appear like this.

Reader feedback

Feedback from our readers is always welcome. Let us know what you think about this book—what you liked or may have disliked. Reader feedback is important for us to develop titles that you really get the most out of.

To send us general feedback, simply send an e-mail to feedback@packtpub.com, and mention the book title via the subject of your message.

If there is a topic that you have expertise in and you are interested in either writing or contributing to a book, see our author guide on www.packtpub.com/authors.

Customer support

Now that you are the proud owner of a Packt book, we have a number of things to help you to get the most from your purchase.

Errata

Although we have taken every care to ensure the accuracy of our content, mistakes do happen. If you find a mistake in one of our books—maybe a mistake in the text or the code—we would be grateful if you would report this to us. By doing so, you can save other readers from frustration and help us improve subsequent versions of this book. If you find any errata, please report them by visiting http://www.packtpub.com/submit-errata, selecting your book, clicking on the **errata submission form** link, and entering the details of your errata. Once your errata are verified, your submission will be accepted and the errata will be uploaded on our website, or added to any list of existing errata, under the Errata section of that title. Any existing errata can be viewed by selecting your title from http://www.packtpub.com/support.

Piracy

Piracy of copyright material on the Internet is an ongoing problem across all media. At Packt, we take the protection of our copyright and licenses very seriously. If you come across any illegal copies of our works, in any form, on the Internet, please provide us with the location address or website name immediately so that we can pursue a remedy.

Please contact us at copyright@packtpub.com with a link to the suspected pirated material.

We appreciate your help in protecting our authors, and our ability to bring you valuable content.

Questions

You can contact us at questions@packtpub.com if you are having a problem with any aspect of the book, and we will do our best to address it.

1
User Management and User Profiling

Salesforce.com is a CRM package as well as a **Platform as a Service (PaaS)**. PaaS means the Salesforce platform can be used to build custom applications apart from a CRM. Salesforce.com is a SaaS plus PaaS. **Software as a Service (SaaS)** is used because of its ability to provide an out-of-the-box ruleset to manage CRM core functionalities, and PaaS is used because of the platform that can be used to build business logic through the provided components. The core of any CRM package is the ease with which it provides its administrators the ability to manage a user's profile. As we walk through this chapter, we will explore how easy it is to create, manage, and profile users in the Salesforce.com CRM.

The first common task of an administrator in Salesforce is to create users who will be the end users for the applications. An application in Salesforce is developed by developers, with the help of a design provided by an architect depending on the business requirement gathered by a business consultant. The scope of this book is to discuss the admin capabilities provided by the platform for an administrator and the day in and day out activities of a Salesforce administrator.

For a better understanding of the topics, I would recommend readers to sign up for a free developer account with Salesforce at Salesforce Developers (`https://developer.salesforce.com/en/signup`) and get hands-on with the concepts explained in this book.

License management

As an administrator, I used to wonder where exactly could I find the count of licenses that are currently available and the number of licenses that have been consumed by an organization.

The following screenshot will help us figure this out in our developer instance:

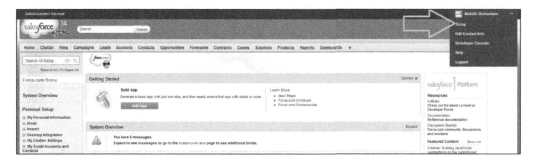

As an administrator, you will find that the **Setup** option (shown in the preceding screenshot) available in the drop-down menu on clicking on your name is very helpful.

Click on your name and navigate to **Setup | Company Profile | Company Information**. Please note that in some production or sandbox instances, the **Setup** link is given next to your name (when logged in using a user's name).

Let's explore the various licenses that your organization can purchase from Salesforce with the help of the following table:

License type	Features and functionalities provided
Salesforce	This is the most comprehensive license and is used to provide users with standard as well as custom CRM functionalities. The advantages are as follows: • Users with this user license are entitled to access any standard or custom app • Each license provides additional storage for Enterprise, Unlimited, and Performance edition users

License type	Features and functionalities provided
Salesforce Platform	This is designed for users who need access to custom apps but not to the standard CRM functionalities. The advantages are as follows: • Users with this user license are entitled to use custom apps developed in your organization or installed from Force.com AppExchange • Users are entitled to use core platform functionalities, such as accounts, contacts, reports, dashboards, documents, and custom tabs
Force. com App Subscription	A Force.com Light App has up to 10 custom objects and 10 custom tabs, read-only access to accounts and contacts, and supports object-level and field-level security

The complete comprehensive list can be referred to at `https://help.salesforce. com/HTViewHelpDoc?id=users_license_types_available.htm&language=en_US`.

It's important to understand the key differences between the Featured and User licenses.

The User license

The **User license** types are assigned to profiles when creating a profile. (We will discuss a profile soon. Until then, let's assume a profile consists of a set of users with the same look and feel for the app and the same functionalities and access).

In Salesforce, a user is required to have a profile. You cannot have a user without a profile. Once a user is assigned a profile, they will inherit the license assigned to that profile. The license that we are referring to here is the User license type.

The Featured license

The **Featured license** is in addition to the normal User license. You will see a small checkbox on the user's record, which means that the user is assigned a Featured license. Common examples of a Featured license are knowledge, content, service cloud, Site.com publisher, and so on. We will explain the functionalities that these licenses provide as we move on.

User management

Let's find out how we can create users in Salesforce. Just navigate to **Setup | Manage Users | Users**.

The **New User** button will open a form, as shown in the following screenshot, to fill in some details. The fields in red are mandatory, and you won't be able to save the information unless and until you fill in these details.

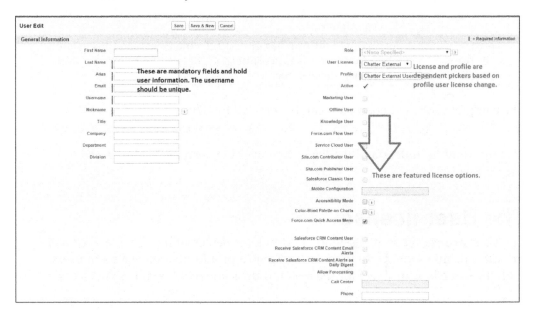

Activating a user

Activating or deactivating a user in Salesforce is just a matter of ticking a checkbox on the user's record.

 The Chatter Free or Chatter Plus license can be upgraded to the Standard full license, but it is not possible the other way round, that is, a full license can't be downgraded to a Chatter Free or Plus license.

Resetting the user password

As an administrator, you will often have e-mails from your application's users to reset their passwords. In the user records page, Salesforce provides a **Reset Password(s)** button to reset a password.

Freezing a user

In some cases, you can't immediately deactivate an account (such as when a user is selected in a custom hierarchy field). To prevent users from logging into your organization while you perform the steps to deactivate them, you can freeze the user's accounts. You will learn more about what a custom hierarchy field is as soon as we explore the database relationship concepts in *Chapter 2, Configuring Salesforce*.

Resetting a user's e-mail address

There are often chances when the e-mail address of your user changes. As an administrator, you can edit a user's record and change it to a new e-mail address. The key point to note here is that the user will have to confirm this once their e-mail address has changed. Salesforce sends an e-mail to the new e-mail address of the user, and the user will be required to confirm the new e-mail address via a link.

Organization-wide password policy

An administrator is not only responsible for creating users but one of the common tasks of an admin is to also maintain the security of the application.

Click on your name and then navigate to **Setup | Security Controls** (under **Administer) | Password Policies**.

You will see some self-explanatory fields on the form to set a password policy.

Expiring all passwords

This is a very sensitive step and one must think twice before expiring every user's password. You can find this option by navigating to **Setup | Security Controls | Expire All Passwords**.

Mobile administration

Salesforce provides some mobile applications out of the box for its users, which can be installed from the App store (for Apple devices) or the Google Play store ( ) (for Android devices). Some of the commonly provided applications are as follows:

- **Salesforce 1**: This app can access most of the functionalities built for a desktop on a mobile and can be customized by your developers. As an admin, you can enable its access to your users and organization.

- **Salesforce For Dashboards**: This app displays dashboards on an iPad or a mobile device that is built for your applications by either an admin or a developer.

- **Salesforce Classic**: This app is a client application that allows access to Salesforce.com data from BlackBerry, iPhone, and Android devices.

A subset of the user's Salesforce information is stored locally on the device, providing access to the user's most critical information even in the absence of a wireless signal.

In addition, the mobile application periodically (and automatically) polls Salesforce.com for new and updated records, ensuring that the device data is always kept up to date. Salesforce Classic provides the user with the ability to view and edit data, track activity history, log calls and e-mails, and view dashboards.

Salesforce Mobile is highly configurable. A custom mobile configuration dictates the overall mobile experience and what objects/tabs, records, and fields are available on the mobile device. If you are asked to configure this application, you can refer online to https://help.salesforce.com/ HTViewHelpDoc?id=mobile_install.htm&language=en_US.

Let's explore where we have to configure all this as an administrator. Click on your name and navigate to **Setup | Mobile Administration**.

Navigation refers to the navigation tabs for Salesforce 1 applications. **Salesforce 1** settings help you configure a new logo and branding for the Salesforce 1 mobile application for your organization. **Salesforce Classic** is the settings option for the Salesforce Classic app. The **Mobile Dashboards** settings are for a mobile dashboard application.

Viewing the login history

Administrators can monitor the successful and failed login attempts for their organization and enabled portals. The columns on this page provide information about each login attempt. The login history page displays the most recent 20,000 entries in the login history database. If you need to see more records, you can download the information to a CSV or GZIP file.

You will find this login history in the user record-related list, as shown in the following screenshot:

Network access and profile-based login IP ranges

To understand this topic, let's explain with the help of the following flowchart how authentication in Salesforce.com works once the user logs in. Under **Profiles**, we can set the **Login Hours** and **Login IP Ranges** options. Similarly, by navigating to **Setup | Security Controls** (under **Administer**) **| Network Access**, you have the option to whitelist some of the IPs.

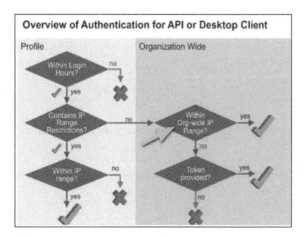

This flowchart is self-explanatory and as you can see, if the restriction is at the profile level, then Salesforce won't allow you to log in.

If your IP range is mentioned in the **Network Access** page, you don't need a security token, which is a self-generated token specific to a user that is needed along with the password to access Salesforce from external client applications (such as Dataloader, Soap UI, and so on).

Profile management

The first question that we must answer and be clear about is "What are profiles in Salesforce?". In the *User Management* section, we explored how to create users in Salesforce. Now, this section will deal with how we profile these users. So, a set of users who will need the same type of object access, tabs, applications, permissions, and user interfaces are categorized into a common profile. This is described in the following screenshot:

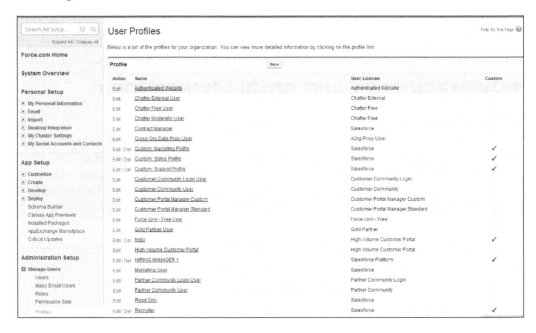

The profiles can be viewed and created by navigating to **Setup | Manage Users | Profiles**.

When a new profile is created, it has to be cloned from the existing profiles. When your organization (org) is purchased from Salesforce, it will already come with some profiles known as standard profiles. One can use these profiles but they are pretty much fixed, and hence we clone them if we need to customize profiles as per our need.

Before I move on, we need to understand applications, objects, fields, tabs, page layouts, and field-level security.

Objects and fields

Just like any other database, Salesforce has its integrated database that comes with the organization once you purchase it. You have the ability to create objects and form fields related to an object through point and click, and hence this eliminates the need for separate database administrators such as PL/SQL.

The creation of these objects and fields can be done via simple clicks and not through any code, and this makes life simpler.

To create objects, you will need to click on your name and navigate to **Setup | Create | Objects**. The sample form to create objects is shown in the following screenshot:

Once you create objects, you can associate fields to them again through point and click. You can assign data types to fields by selecting an option through the radio buttons.

Fields have field-level security that decides whether a profile has API access to a field or not. We will explore this more in the *Configuring a profile* section when we dive deeper.

On the same screen, you will see the **Edit Record Name Label and Format** section. This defines how you want to address your data for an object. For example, if you create an account, it will definitely be addressed by a name, but if you create a transaction receipt, it should be an autogenerated number.

The optional features available on this screen are as follows:

- **Allow Reports**: If you wish to create reports on an object's data, check this flag
- **Allow Activities**: If you wish to create tasks and events related to an object's records, tick this checkbox
- **Track Field History**: If you want to track the changes of any field for an object, turn this flag on

Tabs

Tabs provide a UI to access objects and fill data or records into objects. Objects are like tables in conventional databases and filling data (a layman's language term) is equivalent to inserting rows or records into the objects in Salesforce. For a standard object, we will have default tabs, while for custom objects, tabs have to be created by navigating to **Setup | Create | Tabs**. Again, when we explore more about profiles, we will see how we can hide a tab, keep the default on, or keep the default off for various profiles.

Flexi tabs can be used in Salesforce 1. For more information, refer to `https://help.salesforce.com/HTViewHelpDoc?id=creating_flexipage_tabs.htm&language=en_US`.

Applications

An application will involve a collection of tabs that can be controlled for each profile. Profiles can be configured to give access to only the selected application. You can create apps by navigating to **Setup | Create | Apps**.

Page layouts

The fields that we created for objects are organized to be viewed for various profiles with the help of page layouts. For each profile, we have the option to configure page layouts for that profile.

A page layout is edited with the help of the edit layout link on the page block, which helps us to organize fields and sections. This is shown in the following screenshot:

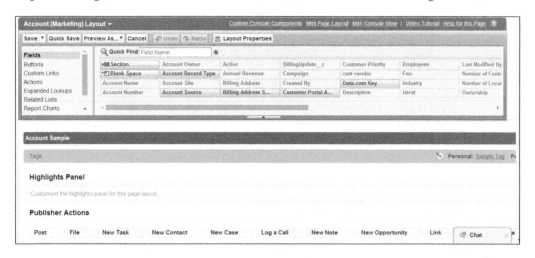

Configuring a profile

Let's navigate to one of the profiles in order to explore the settings that are provided by the profiles, which govern the application.

Click on your name and navigate to **Setup** | **Manage Users** | **Profile**. So, let's scan from the top page of the profile to the bottom and understand the importance of each of the sections.

The Profile Detail, Console Settings, and Page Layouts sections

The **Profile Detail** section consists of the User license that a profile holds. Any user assigned to this profile will inherit the license specified in the profile.

The **Page Layouts** section helps in the page layout assignment. Each profile needs a page layout assignment, and this section helps in assigning the page layout.

The **Console Settings** section is for the console assignment of profiles.

Salesforce console definition and its need

A Salesforce console is designed to boost productivity for users in a fast-paced environment. The console's dashboard-like interface improves the Agent console by eliminating time-consuming clicking and scrolling, so you can quickly find, update, and create records.

The Salesforce console streamlines access to the data and features you need the most. For example, service agents can use multiple applications at once and preserve the context of cases as priorities change. Using the sales console, sales reps can easily contact leads, assess companies, identify key contacts, and access sales intelligence.

- **1**: Select an object to view in the Salesforce console navigation list. For example, select **Leads** to view leads. The administrator can choose which objects are available.
- **2**: Records are displayed in a list, which you can pin on the left or the top of the screen. Select one or more records to be displayed in the primary tabs.
- **3**: Selected records appear in primary tabs. You can work with multiple tabs simultaneously.
- **4**: The highlight panel can be configured separately for each object to show the key information related to the record in the primary tab.
- **5**: Open more than one subtab to quickly switch between multiple related records.
- **6**: View and interact with the subtab content in the detail area.

Field-level security

For each object, standard or custom, the page will consist of various fields. This section will help us configure which fields are visible and which fields are read only at the profile level. Please note that if a field is not visible, it implies that it can't be read only as well. Read only implies that the field cannot be edited even through an API. If the Enhanced Profile User interface is enabled, it will be displayed in **Objects Links** under **Apps**, and then we can select the individual object from there.

Custom app settings and connected app settings

For each profile's details page, you will see the custom app and connected app settings option, and it makes sense not to expose each application to all the profiles. So, this option allows the admin to select the application that should be visible to a profile, and one application can be made default for the profile. The applications that are not checked imply that the users belonging to those profiles won't have access to the unchecked applications at all.

Connected apps provide access to the Salesforce data for external systems (generally for OAUTH 2.0 for mobile apps or external third-party apps). These can also be configured at the profile level similar to the custom app settings:

Tab settings

Tab settings for a profile allow us to control whether the profile has access to the tab or not. There are three selectors: **Default On**, **Default Off**, and **Tab Hidden**.

If the Enhanced Profile User interface is enabled, it will be displayed in **Objects Links** under **Apps**, and then we can select the individual object from there.

Record type settings

Record types allow you to offer different business processes, pick-list values, and page layouts to different users. Record types can be used in various ways. They are as follows:

- You can create record types for opportunities to differentiate your regular sales deals from your professional services engagements and offer different pick-list values for each
- You can create record types for different cases to display different page layouts based on if they are customer support cases or billing cases

The settings at the profile level decide which record types among the available record types should be allocated to the profile. If the Enhanced Profile User interface is enabled, it will be displayed in the **Apps** section.

Administrative permissions and general user permissions

The administrative and general user permissions of profiles provide the capability and access rights for some significant functionalities of the platform. For example, the **View Setup and Configuration** setting will allow users of profiles to view the **Setup** menu. Similarly, **View Encrypted Data** will allow a profile user to view the encrypted fields. The settings are shown in the following screenshot:

Administrative Permissions			
API Enabled	✓	Manage Public List Views	
Chatter Internal User	✓	Manage Public Reports	
Create and Customize List Views	✓	Manage Public Templates	
Create and Own New Chatter Groups	✓	Moderate Communities Feeds	
Edit HTML Templates		Moderate Communities Files	
Invite Customers To Chatter	✓	Password Never Expires	
IP Restrict Requests		Send Outbound Messages	✓
Manage Business Hours Holidays		Tag Manager	
Manage Dashboards		Transfer Record	
Manage Dynamic Dashboards		Use Identity Features	
Manage Entitlements		View Global Header	
Manage External Users		View Help Link	✓
Manage Letterheads		View Setup and Configuration	
Manage Public Documents			

General User Permissions			
Access Custom Mobile Apps		Import Personal Contacts	
Assign Topics	✓	Knowledge One	
Create and Customize Reports	✓	Manage Articles	
Create and Share Links to Chatter Files	✓	Manage Content Permissions	
Create Libraries		Mass Email	✓
Create Topics	✓	Report Builder	

Since the aim of this book is to just explain the concepts, I recommend users to further explore the topic with the help of the *Help & Training* documentation of Salesforce.

Object permissions

For the time being, as we have not discussed the security of the platform, we will not worry much about the **View All** or **Modify All** option. For the objects that we build in Salesforce, we can set whether the profile users can edit the record (**Edit**), have only read access to a record (**Read**), create a record (**Create**), or delete a record from the database (**Delete**). In short, we call it CRUD access.

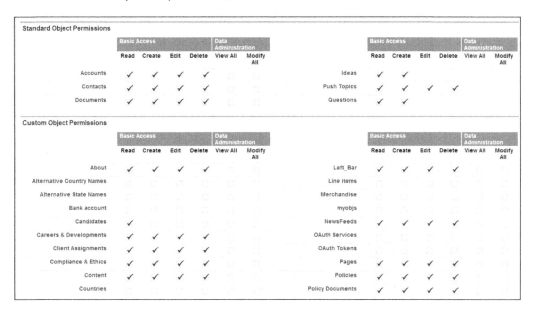

Apex and Visualforce access

Apex and Visualforce are used to customize the business process with code. As an admin, you don't have to go deep into this if you are new to the platform. At the profile level, we can allow these classes and pages if they are needed for a profile.

Note that the login IP restriction and login hours options we discussed are profile-specific. The options for Apex and Visualforce are shown in the following screenshot:

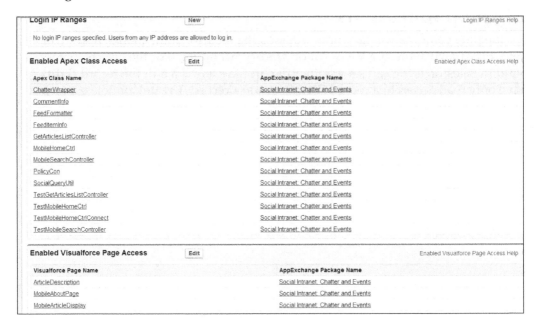

Delegated administration

Delegated administration involves making non-admin users administrators with limited capabilities. Delegated administration will be supported where the users have a role assigned; this means it will support Salesforce Standard and Chatter Only profiles. It will not support Chatter Free and Chatter External profiles as they don't have roles.

The primary functions of a delegated administrator include:

- Creating and editing users and resetting passwords for users in specified roles and all subordinate roles. This also includes setting quotas, creating default opportunity teams, and creating personal groups for those users.
- Unlocking users.
- Assigning users to specified profiles.
- Logging in as a user who has granted login access to the administrator.
- Managing custom objects created by an administrator.

The process starts by navigating to **Setup | Security Controls | Delegated Administration**. The steps are as follows:

1. Create a group and give it a name that is applicable to your business need. If the **Enable Group for Login Access** option is checked, it means that if a user grants login access, the delegated admin can log in on behalf of that user.

2. Assign users who will act as delegated administrators.

3. Specify the roles and subordinates for which the delegated administrators of this group can create and edit users.

4. Specify the profiles that the delegated administrators of this group can assign to the users they create and update. The delegated administrators cannot modify the profile. They can only assign users to these profiles.

5. Specify the custom objects that the delegated administrators of this group can administer. The delegated administrators can manage every aspect of the custom object, except for setting the custom objects' permissions on profiles. All the options are shown in the following screenshot:

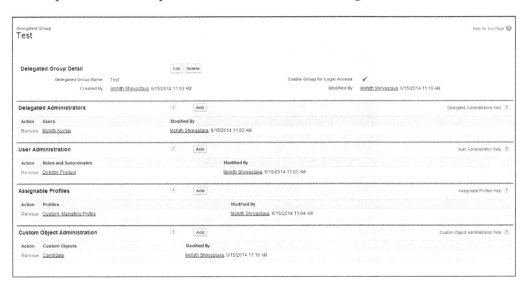

Salesforce A

Salesforce A is a mobile application available on the App Store or the Google Play store on Android devices to administer common admin-related activities from a mobile client.

The Salesforce A mobile app offers greater flexibility for Salesforce administrators. With Salesforce A, you can perform essential user management tasks — including editing user details, resetting passwords, assigning permission sets, and unlocking, freezing, and deactivating user accounts — all from your mobile device. The following is a screenshot of the app:

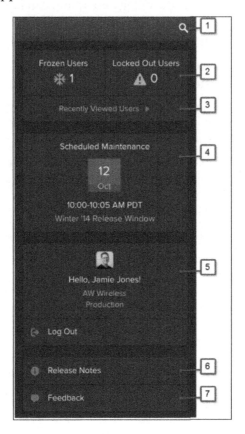

The following explanation helps us figure out how to use the Salesforce A app:

- **1**: Tap on the search box to search for users in your organization. In the search box, type a few letters of a user's name, and then select it from the list that appears.

- **2**: Tap on **Frozen Users** or **Locked Out Users** to open a list of frozen or locked user accounts. From the list, tap on a user to view and edit the user's details.

- **3**: Tap on **Recently Viewed Users** to open a list of users you most recently accessed.

- **4**: View the date, time, and type of the next scheduled maintenance.

- **5**: Verify your username, organization name, and the type of organization you're logged into. Tap on **Log Out** to log out of your account.
- **6**: Tap on **Release Notes** to view the latest release notes in HTML format (The HTML format release notes are currently in beta stage.)
- **7**: Tap on **Feedback** to take a short survey.

Summary

The aim of this chapter was to get acquainted with the profiles and user concepts in Salesforce. The motivation of this chapter was that as an administrator, we understand the platform capabilities provided to profile users, and manage licenses for a user, provide the right access to users, and maintain application access. The topics explained in this chapter included explaining profiles, roles, delegated administration, and the Salesforce A app fundamentals.

If you have not understood the concepts such as record types, page layouts, and so on, there is nothing to worry about as our next chapter will dive deep into these topics with examples. The next chapter will teach you how to build the blocks of Salesforce applications, such as page layout, workflows, approval process, formula fields, building relationships, and so on.

2
Configuring Salesforce

The aim of this chapter is to explain how to approach data modeling in Salesforce and how to map your business rules with the help of some out-of-the-box components provided by Salesforce (through simple clicks). The chapter will explain how some of the form validations can be written with the help of simple validation rules of the Salesforce platform. We will take a look at the configuration components provided out of the box by the platform, which includes page layouts, e-mail templates, workflows, approval processes, formulae, and record types. By the end of the chapter, you will be familiar with building an application using point and clicks.

Data modeling

If you are a database administrator, you will certainly be able to map your existing knowledge to some of the concepts we are going to talk about. However, if you have no database administration experience or prior knowledge, don't worry, as this will require no prerequisites. When I began my career, I had minute knowledge about this platform as well.

So, let's start with a simple day-to-day scenario of credit card transactions that we do online while we are shopping on an online portal. You might have wondered where all the data that you type in the form goes. The answer is a database. A database for a layman is a dark disk or chip where the data resides. Let's be more logical at this point and think from an application's point of view; the database will consist of various objects.

Your organization, once purchased from Salesforce, will already consist of some out-of-the-box objects that are used in normal sales and service processes. You will see that you don't have to do anything to create the account, contact, opportunity, lead, campaign objects, or the case object. Depending on whether you have a feature license or a standard license, you will already see a set of objects, tabs, and apps.

Anything custom (such as custom objects) will require a build; a build here is a point and click. To add a new object and relate it to our existing data model, we will go to the **Build** (**Create** for older orgs) section by navigating to **Setup** | **App Setup** (**Build** for new orgs) | **Create** | **Objects**:

There are four types of relationships possible in Salesforce, which are described in the following table:

Relationship	Key features
Lookup	• A child can be independent and a parent is not mandatory. • Once parent records are deleted, child records will remain in the system and only references will be wiped off. However, we will see that there are some configurations by which we can restrict users from deleting parent records that have child records linked to them.

Relationship	Key features
Master-detail	• Child records mandatorily need a parent record. • Once a parent record is deleted, the child record is automatically deleted. • The child record owner will be the same as the parent record owner. • You can have roll-up summary fields on a parent record, which will display the aggregated count, sum, and max and min of different values from the related child records.
Many-to-many relationships	• Many-to-many relationships need a junction object that has a lookup or master-detail relationship between two objects. We will explore this relationship in detail in the *Many-to-many relationships (concept of a junction object)* section of this chapter.
Hierarchical relationships	• This is a special type of relationship that we will find in a user object. It is used to create a self lookup to the user object itself.

Lookup relationship

As a database administrator, we know that to relate any two tables, we need a foreign key between the two tables (for one-to-many relationships), as depicted in the following screenshot:

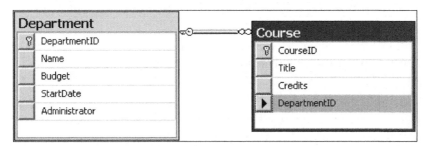

In the table shown in the preceding screenshot, **DepartmentID** is the foreign key and relates the two tables.

From a Salesforce perspective, lookup relationships are defined between two objects by creating a field of the lookup relationship data type on the child, and then selecting the proper parent to establish a relationship between the two objects.

Consider the following steps to link a Department object and a Course object through a simple lookup in Salesforce:

1. Create the `Department` object (let's consider this as the parent object, as shown in the previous screenshot). Navigate to **Setup | Create | Objects** to create this new object.

2. Create the `Course` object (let's consider this as the child object).

3. Create a lookup field on the child object and select the parent object as **Department**. The data type of the field has to be lookup:

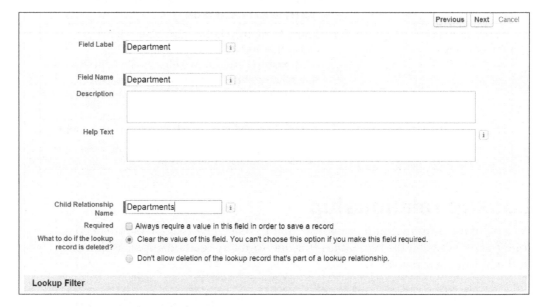

4. In a lookup relationship, we have three major settings. We can create the required lookups that will enforce a user to mandatorily set a parent for any child record.

5. By default, the **Clear the value of this field** option is selected. This means when a parent is deleted, all the associated parent references are deleted from its corresponding child records.

Master-detail relationships

A master-detail relationship is also used to build one-to-many relationships like lookups but the relationship is quite rigid. Rigidity implies the child cannot exist independently of the parent, and once the parent is deleted, the child records are automatically deleted. One of the greatest features of a master-detail relationship is its ability to provide the roll-up summary data type to roll the count or summation of some fields directly onto the parent record. This feature is not possible to use in a lookup relationship.

The procedure to create a master-detail relationship between two objects is very similar to the lookup relationship; just the data type of the field needs to be selected as **Master-Detail Relationship** instead of **Lookup Relationship**:

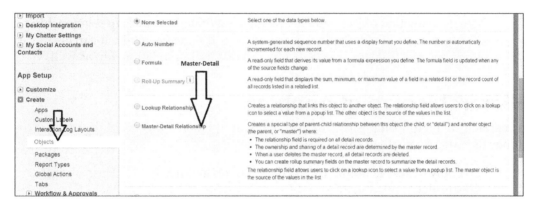

Many-to-many relationships (concept of a junction object)

In a real-life scenario, we often need many-to-many relationships to solve a business problem. Consider an example in which we have sports and players as two objects. A sport can be played by many players; similarly, a player can play more than one sport.

A many-to-many relationship involves defining a third table (called a junction or join table), whose primary key is composed of the foreign keys from both the related tables. In a one-to-one relationship, the primary key acts additionally as a foreign key and there is no separate foreign key column for either table.

In Salesforce, we also define a third table and call it the junction table, which will have any one of the following combinations defined with the other two tables:

- Two lookup relationships
- Two master-detail relationships
- One lookup relationship and one master-detail relationship

It is important to note a few interesting points about this concept. The first master relationship is known as the primary relationship, and it governs the look and feel of the junction records. The steps to create many-to-many relationships are as follows:

1. Create an object named A.
2. Create an object named B.
3. Create a junction object named C, which will have two lookup relationships or two master-detail relationships with A and B, respectively. It can also have one master-detail relationship and one lookup relationship as well.

Hierarchical relationships

A hierarchical relationship is exactly like a lookup relationship, except the only things that are *special* about this relationship are:

- It is only available on the user object with no lookup or master-detail relationship
- It can only look up a user object

Navigate to **User** | **Fields** | **New** and select **Hierarchical Relationship** as the field type.

Now that we have discussed the various relationships, we may want to know where to go in Salesforce to review the schema structure that is built-in (or the one that is already existing in my instance).

The short answer is the schema explorer utility provided by the platform. You can use this to study the schema structure by navigating to **App Setup | Schema Builder**:

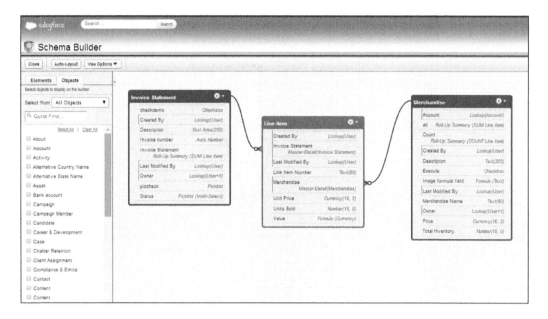

Workflows

Often, our application needs the ability to send e-mail alerts, create and assign tasks on creation and modification of records, or update some of the fields depending on user input.

A common life business scenario could be that on the closure of a case (more specifically, when the status of the **Case** field changes to the value closed), I would like to assign a task to a service rep to inform the customer that their case has been closed and also send an e-mail to the contact (customer) that their case has been resolved.

To achieve all these functionalities, Salesforce has provided us with a toolset named workflows.

To start building a workflow, navigate to **Setup | Create | Workflow & Approvals | Workflow Rules**, as shown in the following screenshot:

The workflow itself has two main parts; I generally call the first part the header and the other part, the action. The header consists of three mandatory parts: rule name, evaluation criteria, and rule criteria. The action will involve four types: primarily field updates, e-mail alerts, tasks, and outbound messages. These actions can be immediate or time dependent. Time dependent means we have the option to execute the workflow action after a certain interval of time (it is configurable ranging from minimum number of hours to maximum number of years).

Let's explore all the information we have collected with the help of a simple example.

The problem statement is that we are going to create a workflow to solve our business problem of sending an e-mail to the contacts on the closure of a case and also create a task against the owner of the case.

Create the header first. As discussed, the header will involve three important aspects:

- Object selection and name
- Evaluation criteria
- Entry criteria

For the evaluation criteria, one has to make a choice between three different types with the help of a radio button. The types are as follows:

- **created**
- **created, and every time it's edited** (a time dependent action is not possible using this type)
- **created, and any time it's edited to subsequently meet criteria**

The third option implies that the workflow will not always fire. It will fire only if there is a change made that affects the rule criteria.

Let's consider the last option for our example.

Rule Criteria is a simple formula-based expression or logical expression that is necessary to be satisfied for the action to be triggered.

In our scenario, the **Rule Criteria** is that the **Status** field of **Case** should be **Closed**. This is shown in the following screenshot:

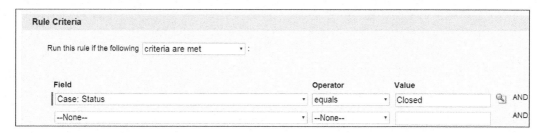

After entering data for the header, let's associate some actions to the workflow rule. The actions for our problem will be e-mail alerts and task creation.

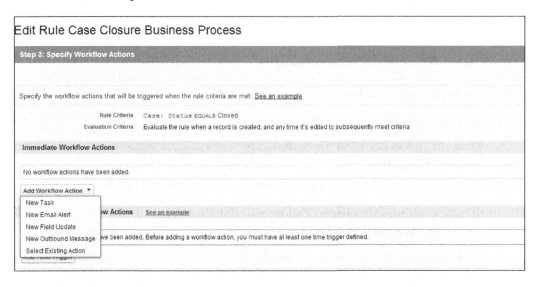

Our task will be to create an e-mail alert and an action for the creation of a new task. For a new task, you will need to fill in a form, which looks similar to the following screenshot:

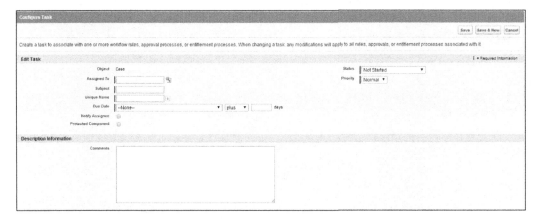

The **Assigned To** field will be the case owner selected from the lookup icon. Our next section will deal with e-mail alerts.

For a **time-dependent workflow**, we will need to add a time trigger as well as defining the workflow action.

To see the entire configuration in action, you will need to go to the **Cases** tab, edit a case, and bring it to the **Closed** status. Then, you will receive an e-mail alert and an activity will be assigned as per the form details for the new task we created in the previous step.

Another very important concept to understand is how to monitor time-dependent workflows in Salesforce. Navigate to **Setup | Administration Setup | Monitoring | Time-Based Workflow** to access the **Time-Based Workflow** window. This is shown in the following screenshot:

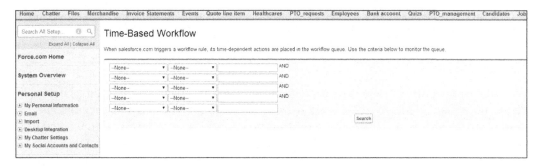

Here, on selecting certain parameters from the dropdown, you will be able to search for a time-based workflow and see its status. If you do not enter any search criteria, it will display all the scheduled actions on the same page.

It's again important to understand that if the rule parameter variables change (that is, **Field** values) in the time period for which the workflow action is in a time-dependent queue, the time-dependent action readjusts itself.

E-mail templates

E-mail templates determine the look and feel and also the content or the body of the e-mail that goes out of Salesforce. One of the greatest abilities of the e-mail templates is to dynamically associate the data of a record with the e-mail that's flowing out of the Salesforce system.

E-mail templates are stored under public folders called unified folders, or your personal folder or a custom-created folder. For the time being, let's not worry too much about the folders and assume we are creating a new e-mail template from the unified public folder. You can create the e-mail template by navigating to **Setup | Administration Setup | Communication Templates | Email Templates**. There are basically four different types of options that we will see when we create an e-mail template.

The options are shown in the following screenshot:

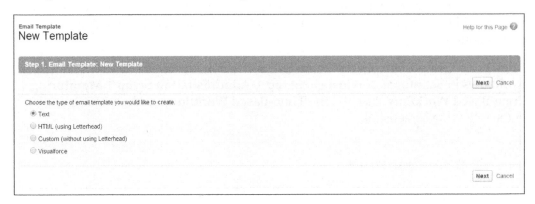

We will be concentrating on how to make a quick HTML-based e-mail template. Please note that HTML templates are usually delivered by a design agency or the marketing department. This is not a part of the job role of an administrator. Before we use an HTML (with a letterhead) type of template, it's important to create the letterhead itself. To create a letterhead, navigate to **Setup | Administration Setup | Communication Templates | Letterheads**.

The creation of letterheads is simple. There are some sections that need to be populated. They will consist of an interface for the header logo, body, footer logo, header properties for a thick border line, and body color to make the letterhead look professional.

The following screenshot shows the letterhead format that you will need to configure for your organization:

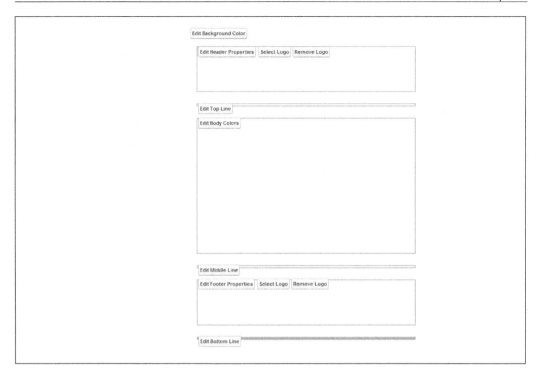

Once we have a letterhead ready, it is just a matter of associating the letterhead with the e-mail template, as shown in the following screenshot:

The relevant content can be placed in the placeholder using the merge field concept in Salesforce. Merged fields make the content dynamic, and they pull data from records for fields specified as merge fields. This is shown in the following screenshot:

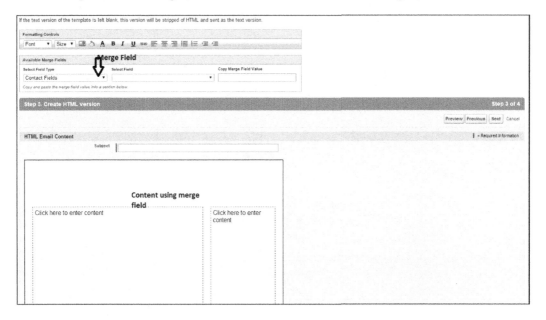

The merge fields concept uses bracket notation, and during runtime, these fields will automatically derive contents from the respective fields. For example, if I have a merge field with the notation {!Case.CaseNumber}, the case number for each record will be replaced in the e-mail template for each case for which an e-mail will flow.

The **Available Merge Fields** section helps to generate the syntax for merge fields that we can use. Also, the editor is a rich text editor, which helps to format the font and also insert images if needed into the e-mail templates.

For those interested in going step by step and need more clarity, you can refer to http://www.wikihow.com/Create-an-Email-Template-in-Salesforce.

Approval process

In the time we spend at the office, we are all confronted with processes that require approvals. An approval can be for a leave application from your manager. For a few organizations, an approval can be for expenses or orders. Here, an expense, order, or leave is a record in our object (either standard or custom) for which we need approval.

An approval process specifies the steps necessary for a record to be approved and who must approve it at each step. A step can apply to all records included in the process, or just records that meet certain administrator-defined criteria. An approval process also specifies the actions to be taken when a record is submitted, approved, rejected, and recalled. Let's configure an approval process for a business problem that says for all merchandise with a price of $50 and above, approval is required from the manager but if the price is over $5,000, the approval needs to be from a Vice President (VP). Let's assume we will use a standard wizard to create our process.

The following are the questions that one must be familiar with before configuring the approval process:

- What is the entry criteria that the approval process must follow?

  The approval process must follow the formula expression that uses fields or related fields of the record.

- Who should be the next automated approver?

  The answer to this will be either the manager of the logged-in user or a custom hierarchical field of the user, which is selected as per our wish. We can also automatically select a checkbox to consider the owner's manager or hierarchical field. This is done by default and when we take a stab at the steps, we can override it to include specific users and queues.

- What are the record editability properties?

  The answer to this will be that either only the admin or the admin and the current approver can edit the field. The approval assignment e-mail template needs to be kept ready to be assigned to the approval process.

- What are the devices from which the approver can approve or reject the record?

  We can set the approver device option using a radio button, as shown in the following screenshot:

Security Settings

- ⦿ Allow approvers to access the approval page only from within the salesforce.com application. (Recommended)
- ◯ Allow approvers to access the approval page from within the salesforce.com application, or externally from a wireless-enabled mobile device. ⓘ

- Who can be defined as initial submitters?

  Initial submitters can be portal users, users, owners, or members of specific public groups or separate roles, as shown in the following screenshot:

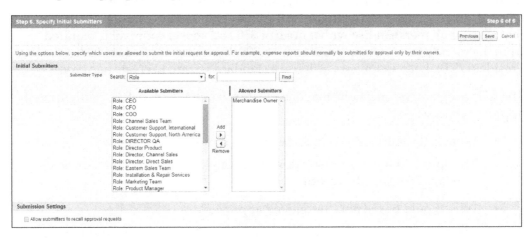

We will now look into the approval steps for which our approval process needs to be configured. Approval steps also include some configuration. The configuration will involve the following steps:

1. First, we require a step number for the step.

2. Then, we will need a step criteria similar to the formula criteria we have seen so far. This is shown in the following screenshot:

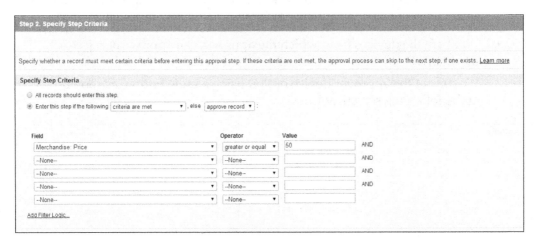

3. Next, we have the option to select the approver, as shown in the following screenshot. This may be a little confusing, but remember, this is just an override to the next selected automated approver we have seen during the process.

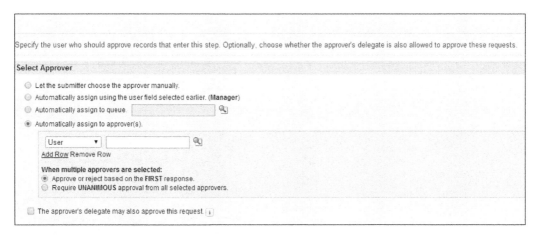

4. The next step is to create approval actions for this step and similarly, one can create multiple steps as per business rules. In our case, we will need just two steps. One to submit the approval to the manager and another to the VP with different rule criteria, and then approval actions depending on the need to send an e-mail, assign a task, update a field, or send an outbound message to an external system.

5. One thing we need to decide is the final action after the final rejection and the final approval. Recall actions are used, for example, if at any stage the user needs to recall the approval process (more like deciding not to submit the record). This needs to be configured as well.

   One crucial thing is that in a multistep process, we have another important option to send the record to a recent approver once the original approver rejects it, as shown in the following screenshot:

Once your flow is ready, you will see the it as shown in the following screenshot:

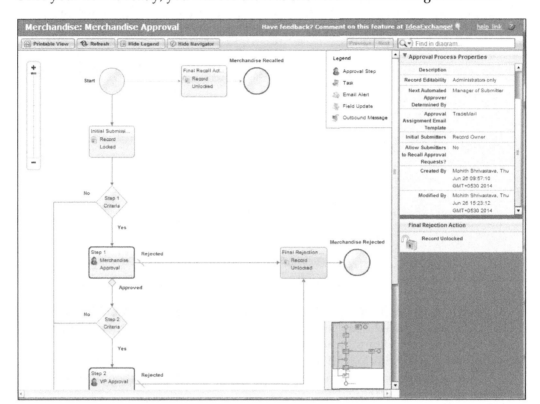

One has to add the **Submit for Approval** button to the page layout, and then click on this button to submit the record for approval. Once this is done, the record is locked from further edits. A user can also configure approval layouts. Approval layouts show fields that the user can view when they are approving/rejecting a record.

Page layouts

Page layouts are generally quick configurable layouts, where the admin arranges the fields in various sections. The page layout can be adjusted by dragging and dropping the available fields in the various sections of the page. To arrange the fields on a page layout, as an admin, you will find an **Edit Layout** link at the top of the standard page in Salesforce. Alternatively, you can go the **Object** page. It has a related list called **Page Layout**. Click on the **Edit** link.

The following screenshot shows the page where you can define page layouts:

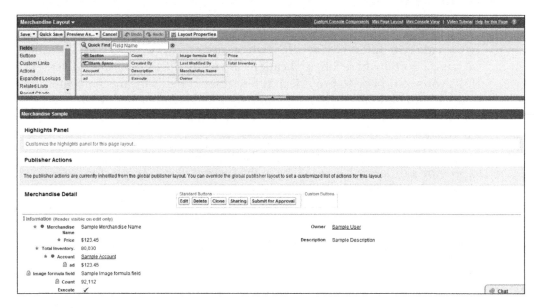

The preceding screenshot shows how you can drag different fields to their respective sections.

A very important point to remember is that we can have more than one page layout for an object, and we can associate different page layouts to profiles as per record type. We will discuss each record type in detail in the next section.

Page layouts will have page layout assignments at the profile level to be assigned to the respective profiles and record types. Refer to *Chapter 1, User Management and User Profiling*, to see how this is done at the profile level.

At the page layout level, you can make some fields mandatory if needed by clicking on the spanner icon, as shown on the right-hand side of the following screenshot, and ticking the **Required** checkbox:

The difference with field-level security (FLS) is that in FLS, a mandatory field won't be available on the API (for example, Dataloader), while the page layout makes the field mandatory or read-only at the UI layer itself.

Record types

We need record types usually for the following two purposes:

- To provide two different views for two or more separate processes. Assume we have a portal where job applications are being filled in by candidates. Now, you would like to provide a different set of fields for mechanical engineering candidates and a different set of fields for an electronics engineer. To achieve this, we allocate different page layouts to different record types.

- Another use case is when we have picklists and for each process, you need to provide a different set of values in the picklist. For example, for the mechanical engineer job application form, you don't need to ask subjects (assuming the subject is a field on the object to indicate the final year subjects that are under the curriculum) such as Analog or Digital. Similarly, for electronics subjects, you cannot display picklists that are irrelevant to the electronics stream.

Every object will have a record type link to create different record types, as shown in the following screenshot:

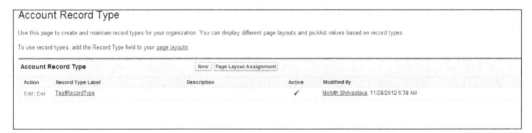

As shown in the preceding screenshot, there is a button to assign a page layout for the record types with various profiles. Have a look at the following screenshot:

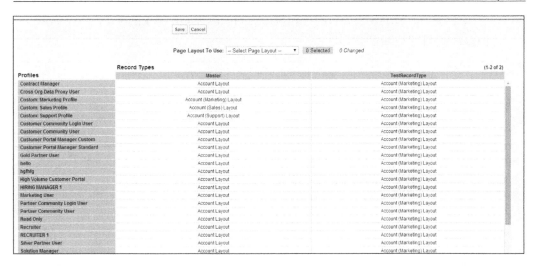

This is a kind of a matrix interface to associate page layouts with various record types as per each profile.

The concept of sales and support processes provided is based on record types, and we will discuss this when we dive deep into it later in this book.

The following configuration is the most common place where, as an admin, you will end up once you need to assign different picklists for a record type of a particular profile. The steps are as follows:

1. Navigate to the profile through **Setup | Manage Users | Profiles**.
2. Navigate to the record type settings.

3. Click on the **Edit** link on one of the objects to assign picklists for the record type of a particular profile:

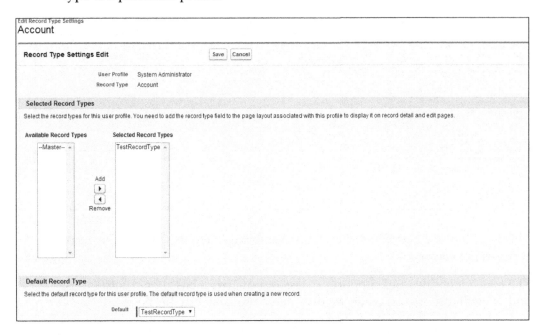

Formulae

I am sure you know the importance of formulae in Mathematics or Physics, thanks to which our tasks have become simpler. We just provide the input and expect an output without diving deep into the logical statements. However, being in the IT world, logic is a part of day-to-day activities. If you have used MS Excel, you will know how helpful formulae are, especially VLOOKUP, Transpose, and so on.

For the workflow criteria, approval process criteria, formula fields, validations, and many more scenarios, you will come across an advanced formula editor, which will provide you with the ability to write some logic using the merge fields concept, and some common logical and mathematical operators, text, date, and so on.

For a comprehensive list, I would recommend that you refer to the document at https://help.salesforce.com/HTViewHelpDoc?id=customize_functions. htm&language=en_US.

The formula editor will look as shown in the following screenshot. It is available when you create a formula field or write a workflow criteria:

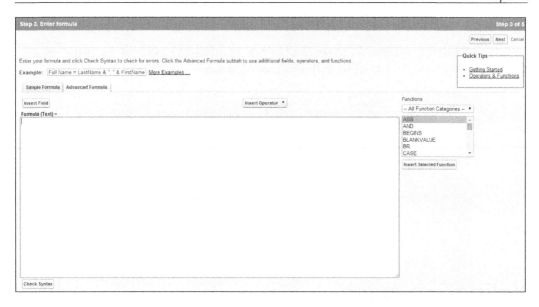

As shown in the editor in the preceding screenshot, you can insert fields using the menu on the left and apply functions for logic using the menu titled **Functions** on the right. You can read the documentation to find some example cases. Some simple use cases will be to check whether the entered data is a number or not.

For more information on different types of functions and operators, refer to https://help.salesforce.com/ HTViewHelpDoc?id=customize_functions_a_h. htm&language=en_US and https://help.salesforce. com/HTViewHelpDoc?id=customize_functions_i_z. htm&language=en_US.

It's out of the scope of this book to dive into each of the functions but believe me, it's not so difficult once you go through the syntax of all the functions. It's similar to an Excel formula and the Boolean AND, NOT, and OR gate logic. Let me draft a formula for IF, as it is widely used. The syntax will be very simple and similar to how we use it in Excel.

The syntax is IF(logical_test, value_if_true, value_if_false). Replace logical_test with the expression you want evaluated, value_if_true with the value you want returned if the expression is true, and value_if_false with the value you want returned if the expression is false.

A common example could be as follows:

Use the default value formula to set the tax rate of an asset based on the user's city. Create a custom percent field with the following default values:

```
IF($User.City = "Napa", 0.0750,
 IF($User.City = "Paso Robles", 0.0725,
  IF($User.City = "Sutter Creek", 0.0725,
   IF($User.City = "Los Olivos", 0.0750,
    IF($User.City = "Livermore", 0.0875, null
    )
   )
  )
 )
)
```

Validation rules

Validation is important to keep the records clean and avoid users from entering junk data. Salesforce provides the ability to validate data of each record that can be written in a formula to prevent users from entering wrong or unwanted data. Validation uses the formula we discussed to check for the error scenario. The error can be thrown at the global level (page level) and the field level.

The navigation path for the validation rule for a standard object is **Setup | Customize | [Object Name] | Validation Rules**. Alternatively, for newer orgs, we can also it find through **Build | Accounts | Validation Rules**. The navigation path for the validation rule for a custom object is **Setup | Objects | Validation Rules**.

Let's draft a validation rule now to restrict users to only enter numbers in the **AccountNumber** standard field (note that as it's a standard text field, we cannot change the data type to a number and avoid this rule).

So, the hint is to use the ISNUMBER function; let's see how in the **Salesforce.com (SFDC)** interface, you can achieve this:

As shown in the preceding screenshot, it's quite evident that the error message is displayed in the field. The interface provides us with the option to write our own custom message, as shown in the following screenshot:

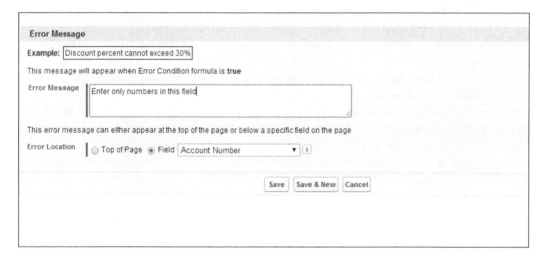

Another advantage is that you can activate and deactivate these rules at any time by just ticking a checkbox named **Active** present on the page. The following screenshot clearly shows the error message that the user will receive if he/she inputs non-numerical characters in the field:

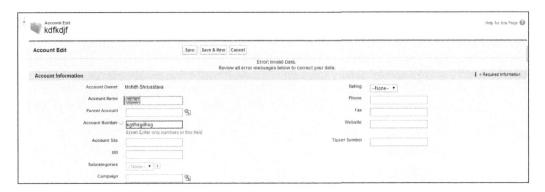

Summary

So, there is a lot you learned in this chapter. Small applications have fewer components, while an enterprise application may have a huge number of objects, page layouts, different types of record types for most of the objects, validation rules, complex formulae, workflows, approval processes, and sophisticated data models. A good understanding of this chapter will help you decide which components have to be used for what purpose. After understanding this chapter, you will be empowered with the components and toolsets that are needed to build small scale to large scale applications through just a click. Although code is part of development, an administrator must be familiar with the configuration utilities provided by the platform to solve business problems. Anything that's beyond a click opens scope for code, and that's where the developer role comes into the picture.

In the next chapter, we will discuss various types of reports and dashboards. The analytical capabilities of the platform play a significant role in administration.

3
Reports and Dashboards

The aim of this chapter is to explain the capabilities of reports and dashboards of the Salesforce platform. Data visualization helps to communicate information clearly and effectively through graphical means. The reports and dashboards feature provided by the Salesforce platform empowers administrators to make reports on the Salesforce data. To build sophisticated reports on the platform, one has to rely on development efforts using the Visualforce technology of Salesforce or the analytics API, or using tools such as QlikView or Tableau. The report builder is still an important utility, and once mastered by an admin, it can be used to build some basic and medium-complexity reports. As we explore more on reports in this chapter, we will see different types of reports, the usage of custom report types, dashboards, analytic snapshots on the platform, and some important formulae functions that can be used on reports, such as PARENTGROUPVAL and PREVGROUPVAL.

The report builder

Let's familiarize ourselves with the report builder in **Salesforce.com** (**SFDC**). Navigate to the **Reports** tab in SFDC by clicking on the + symbol next to all the tabs (the symbol that's used to view all the other tabs, which are by default off).

As shown in the following screenshot, on clicking the **Reports** tab, a screen will be displayed where there are predefined folders; on clicking each folder, you will see various reports. Most of them are standard and they come out of the box. It's important to explore these reports so that they can be modified or adopted for your business process.

The following screenshot shows the page view once the user has navigated to the **Reports** tab:

To create a new folder, click on the folder icon, as shown in the following screenshot:

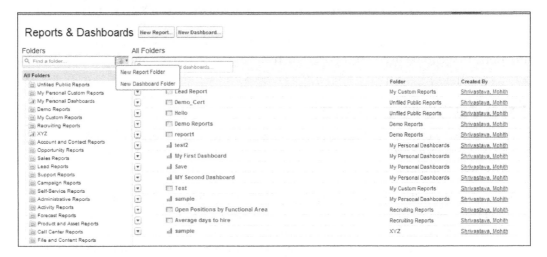

 Note that there needs to be separate folders to hold reports and dashboards.

To make searching for various folders simpler, there is a simple search icon, which is present both at the folder and report level.

There are four possible types of reports one can have, which are as follows:

- Tabular report
- Summary report
- Matrix report
- Joined report

Tabular reports

This is a very basic type of report, where we will be able to tabulate data from objects and other related objects. The maximum number of rows that will be returned by a report is 2,000 records. The steps for the creation of reports are as follows:

1. Click on the **Reports** tab and then click on the **New Report** button, as shown in the following screenshot:

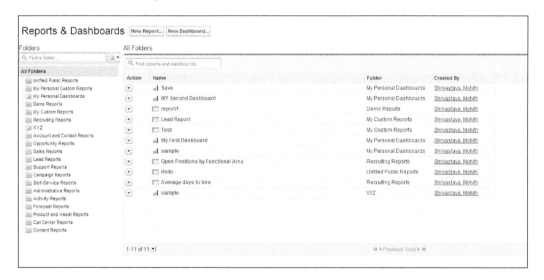

2. Click on the object for which the report needs to be created.
3. Then, click on the **Create** button to start drafting tabular reports.

The following screenshot illustrates the steps to draw a tabular report for all opportunities in our organization. In this process, we will dive deeper into each of the components of the report builder that's provided.

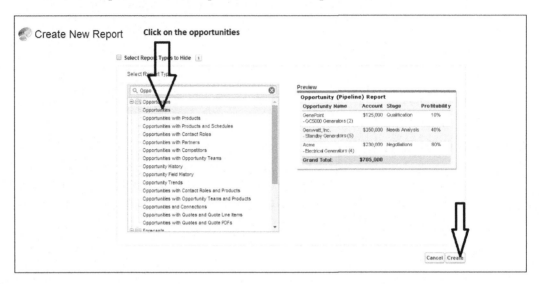

Report builder components

For the data that has been displayed in the preceding screenshot, one can apply various filters such as **Field Filter**, **Cross Filter**, and **Row Limit**. They are described as follows:

- **Field Filter**: This implies filtering data based on the field values. An example could be filtering only opportunities that are closed-won. Closed-won opportunities are the ones that the sales rep has successfully won. This will require a simple field filter at the field opportunity stage.

- **Cross Filter**: This implies selecting data with or without the associated child records. For example, for opportunities, one can have them with or without activities.

- **Row Limit**: This implies applying sorting of the records with specific fields along with limiting the number of rows. Let's say I need the top 20 opportunities among all the opportunities; I will add a row limit with **Opportunity Amount** as the field and the limit number as 20.

The following screenshot shows the different types of filters that are possible on reports:

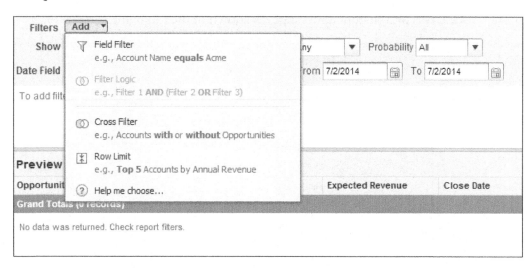

Data visibility in reports

We will discuss more on data visibility in *Chapter 4, Record-level Access, Security, and Audit Features*; however, for now, let's understand that to pull data related to visibility or security (role hierarchy, which we will explore later), we have a filter in the report builder as shown in the following screenshot. The **Show** variable in the report builder defines data that should be pulled for reports, whether it's as per **My team**, **My**, or for **All**. This depends on who the end user of this report will be; for example, for the VP (Vice President) of a company, we will show a report on all opportunities. If it's only for the sales representative, it is advisable to only show his/her opportunities or opportunities that he/she owns (my opportunities). The options shown in the following screenshot will be available for all objects, but the option values won't match exactly. For example, if you are creating a report on a custom object, the team options won't be present.

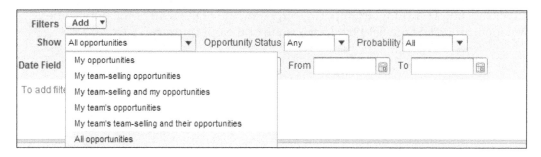

The Date Field filter

The **Date Field** filter will be applied to date variables and data will be filtered per quarter, fiscal year, or a custom date range, as shown in the following screenshot:

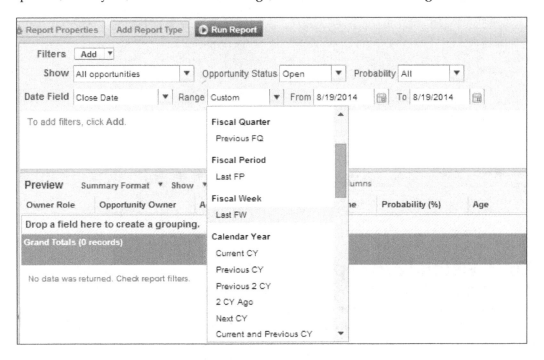

Summary reports

Let's extend the tabular report we have built so far to create a summary report. All that's needed is to start grouping the report by **Stage** or any other relevant field. We will build the summary formula field, which will help us calculate the average and sum for each column (for the number, percent, and currency fields only).

One has to drag a field to the top row to achieve grouping. The following screenshot shows a summary report grouped by the **Stage** field of the opportunity. An opportunity's **Stage** field tracks the stage of the opportunity.

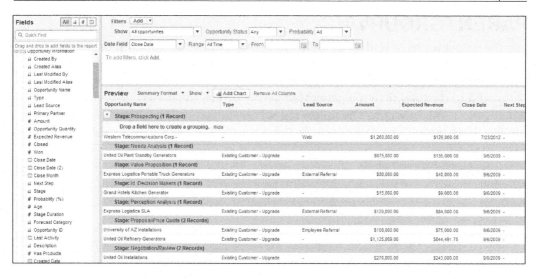

In summary reports, the greatest advantage is that we can summarize a column, as shown in the following screenshot. For example, if we want to summarize the opportunity amount for each stage, we will group the report by each stage and then summarize it.

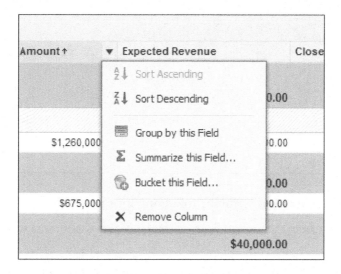

There are two important functions in report formulae, which are given less importance but have a greater utility. They are PARENTGROUPVAL and PREVGROUPVAL.

PARENTGROUPVAL

For the report we have built so far, we are going to show the amount or revenue generated with respect to the total yearly amount for each month (as a percentage). For example, the percentage of the contribution of opportunities each month compared to the total revenue generated yearly can be calculated using the PARENTGROUPVAL function. The following screenshot shows the expected revenue that has been added as a column in the report using the PARENTGROUPVAL formula:

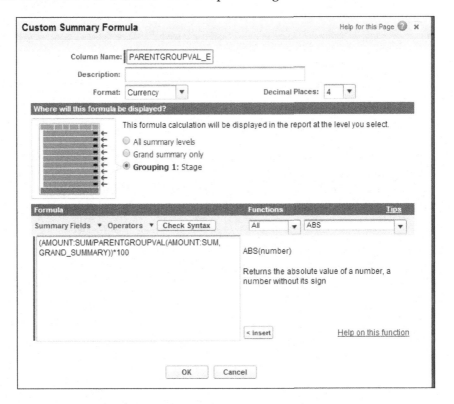

Open the formula editor and write the following formula:

```
(AMOUNT:SUM/PARENTGROUPVAL(AMOUNT:SUM, GRAND_SUMMARY))*100
```

It's important to understand the formula's end results. This formula yields the percentage contribution of the opportunity amount in each month to the total amount or revenue generated yearly.

 For more information on PARENTGROUPVAL, watch the video at https://www.youtube.com/watch?v=7pn-9yCLgRE.

This is useful to calculate the amount of opportunities for each month with respect to the yearly total. The PARENTGROUPVAL formula helps to find the relative percentage of each grouping with respect to the parent sum obtained after the grouping.

PREVGROUPVAL

You can use the PREVGROUPVAL function to calculate values relative to a peer grouping. If there's no peer grouping, the function will return a null value.

This function provides the value for the peer grouping on the same hierarchy level. This allows you to prepare reports that show, for example, a month-to-month opportunity comparison.

Please note that these functions are also applicable to the matrix report type that we will be diving into next.

An example PREVGROUPVAL formula may look as follows:

```
AMOUNT:SUM - PREVGROUPVAL(AMOUNT:SUM, CLOSE_DATE)
```

The preceding formula calculates how the opportunity amount has progressed month-wise. The difference or trend between each month can be calculated using the PREVGROUPVAL function. The report has been assumed to be grouped by **Close Date**, as shown in the following screenshot:

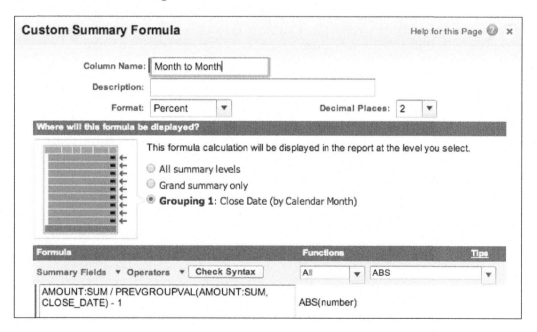

The following screenshot displays the **Month To Month** column added to a report formed using the `PREVGROUPVAL` function:

		Amount	Month to Month
	Close Date: June 2011 **(2 records)**	€550,000.00	
	Close Date: July 2011 **(2 records)**	€240,000.00	-56.36 %
	Close Date: August 2011 **(1 record)**	€40,000.00	-83.33 %
	Close Date: September 2011 **(2 records)**	€90,000.00	125.00 %
	Close Date: November 2011 **(1 record)**	€20,000.00	-77.78 %
	Grand Totals (8 records)	€940,000.00	

Matrix reports

With the term **matrix**, we can imagine both columns and rows. Matrix reports allow us to group at both the row and column levels. A summary report can be converted into a matrix report by selecting **Matrix** from **Report Type** from the summary report. Let's convert our summary report that we have created so far to the matrix format, as shown in the following screenshot:

		Lead Source										Grand Total	
Stage		-	Web	Phone Inquiry	Purchased List	Word of mouth	Employee Referral	External Referral	Partner	Public Relations	Trade Show		Type
Prospecting	Sum of Expected Revenue Sum of Age Record Count	$0.00 0 0	$126,000.00 781 1	$2,280,700.00 782 1	$0.00 0 0	$0.00 0 0	$0.00 0 0	$0.00 0 0	$0.00 0 0	$0.00 0 0	$0.00 0 0	$2,406,700.00 1,563 2	
Western Telecommunications Corp.-	Expected Revenue Age		$126,000.00 781 1										-
Jackson Controls-	Expected Revenue Age			$2,280,700.00 782 1									-
Qualification	Sum of Expected Revenue Sum of Age Record Count	$0.00 996 1	$0.00 0 0	$0.00 0 0	$0.00 0 0	$0.00 0 0	$0.00 0 0	$0.00 0 0	$0.00 0 0	$0.00 0 0	$0.00 0 0	$0.00 996 1	
name	Expected Revenue Age	- 996 1											-
Needs Analysis	Sum of Expected Revenue Sum of Age Record Count	$135,000.00 1,011 1	$0.00 0 0	$0.00 0 0	$0.00 0 0	$0.00 0 0	$0.00 0 0	$0.00 0 0	$0.00 0 0	$0.00 0 0	$0.00 0 0	$135,000.00 1,011 1	
United Oil Plant Standby Generators	Expected Revenue Age	$135,000.00 1,011 1											Existing Customer - Upgrade
Value Proposition	Sum of Expected Revenue	$0.00	$0.00	$0.00	$0.00	$0.00	$125,000.00	$40,000.00	$0.00	$0.00	$0.00	$165,000.00	

We have changed our summary report into a matrix report and grouped it by a column. Here, we have **Lead Source** as the grouping column:

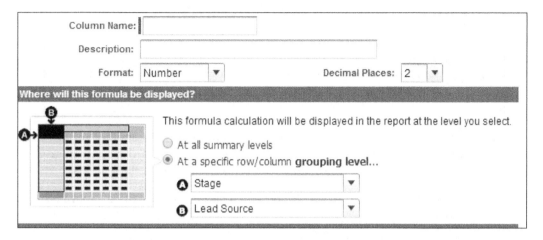

The preceding screenshot shows the report's formula field that gives us the option to display the data at both the row and column level. Also, the PREVGROUPVAL and PARENTGROUPVAL formula functions are also applicable to matrix reports.

Joined reports

Joined reports can create a join between either two summary reports, a summary and matrix report, or two matrix reports. Each report forms a subreport that can be sorted or filtered. The add-on feature of a joined report is so that each report can be based on two different report types. Have a look at the following screenshot:

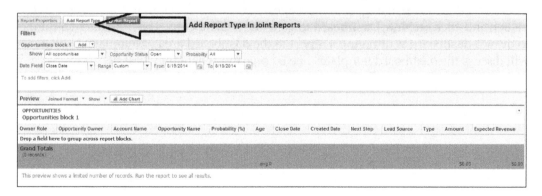

The first thing to observe in a joined report is that we have the **Add Report Type** button enabled; hence, we can add one more report type and join it to the existing report. So, joined reports are two different reports merged into one report.

 The groupings of joined reports remain unaltered if you decide to change from a summary report to a joined report. If matrix reports are converted to joined reports, the same effect in grouping is observed similar to the observation that is made when matrix reports are converted to summary reports.

An example of a joined report is our existing report merged with another report, let's say, another account report. The common fields have to be dropped in an area, as shown in the previous screenshot, and both reports can access these fields.

Up to five different reports can be combined and a single report can be generated from joined reports.

All these reports (tabular, summary, matrix, and joined) cannot display data of more than 2,000 rows. This is an important limitation of Salesforce reporting, and you always have the option to use the **Export Details** button to export the complete data.

Dashboards

Dashboards are an important means of visualization of data. For management activities, dashboards provide a quick estimation to track progress. We will soon see that the prerequisites to build dashboards are reports. Reports form the source for the dashboards.

To create a dashboard, navigate to the **Reports** tab as discussed in the *The report builder* section and click on **New Dashboard** to generate a dashboard. The fundamental thing to draw a dashboard is dragging a report to the dashboard area or template. Now, we will discuss the dashboard templates one by one and where they best fit.

The following screenshot illustrates various types of dashboard components:

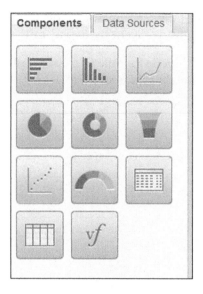

The various types of dashboard components are as follows:

- Bar charts (vertical and horizontal)
- Line charts
- Pie charts
- Donut charts
- Funnel charts
- Scatter charts
- Gauge charts
- Metric charts
- Tabular charts

Bar charts

Bar charts are used when we have a summary report with a single grouping or when we have multiple groupings but we want to display only one grouping on the graph.

The following screenshot is a good example of a bar graph, where it shows the total number of opportunities against various stages:

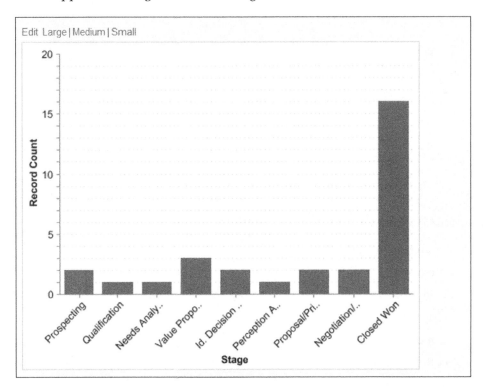

Line charts

Line charts show changes in the value of an item over a period of time. Line charts are used when we have an ordered set of groupings for one item and the other item to be displayed in the chart can be shown over this ordered item.

For example, to see the number of leads converted each month in a report, we can set the converted lead count as the y axis and the month as the x axis. The chart displays a line connecting the record count totals for each month, as shown in the following screenshot. Salesforce does not plot missing (null) values.

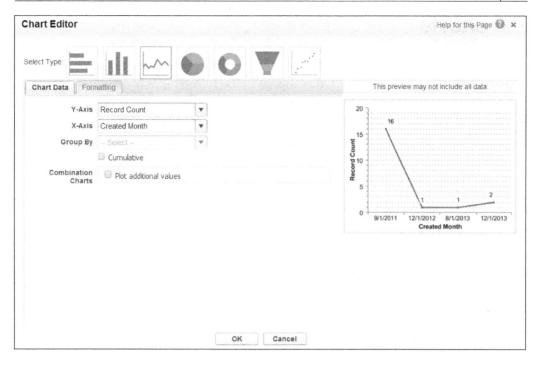

Using the **Chart Editor** window, we can plot a line chart for the example discussed, and the final dashboard is as shown in the following screenshot. Observe that the **Chart Editor** window has an option to format, and one can format the charts appropriately using the formatter.

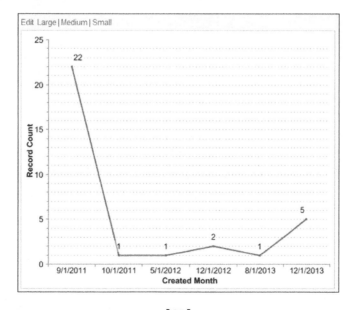

Pie charts

Pie charts are used when we want to show the contribution of individual grouped records against the total. The pie chart for the same requirement as discussed in the previous section is shown in the following screenshot. The procedure remains the same; drag the same report that we developed into the pie chart type dashboard component.

Donut charts

The difference between a donut chart and a pie chart is that a donut chart shows the total amount as well, whereas the pie chart behavior is showing only the percentage individual contribution against the total. An example donut chart is shown in the following screenshot:

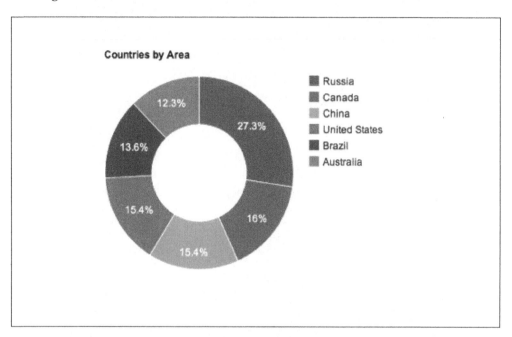

Funnel charts

Funnel charts are used when you have multiple groupings in an ordered set and you want to show proportions among them.

To see the number of opportunities in each stage in a report, set **Amount** as **Values** and **Stage** as **Segments**. As the **Opportunity: Stage** field is an ordered picklist, the stages are sorted in the same order as the picklist, with each segment representing the amount for that stage. Funnel charts can give a rough idea on how opportunities have flowed through the stages.

Select **Show Labels**, **Show Values**, or **Show Segment** % to include the respective information on the chart. A funnel chart is shown in the following screenshot:

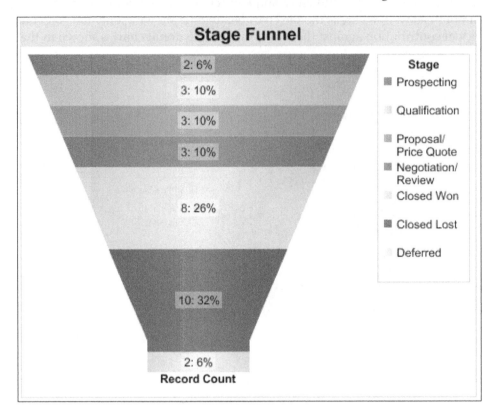

Scatter charts

Remember to use a scatter chart when you need the following:

- Information using one or two groups of report data
- Summary plotting related to each grouping
- To study the correlation between two parameters

The following screenshot shows the scatter graph of **Lead Status** and opportunity amounts, which is grouped by **Lead Status**. This will identify which mode of lead gathering produced more opportunities.

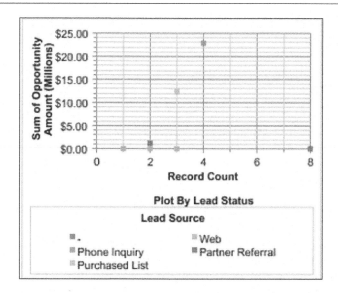

Metric charts

Metric charts are often used to sum different values of a report and assign an appropriate label to it. One can have a metric that is named revenue target for the month, which may include the sum of the total amount for all the opportunities in the closed, commit, and base case stages in the current month.

We will need to make two choices for our dashboards that we build:

1. Select the dashboard component type from the mentioned dashboard types.
2. Select the source report for your dashboard component (most of them need summary reports with a grouping and also with at least one column summarized)

Procedure for conditional highlighting

We can highlight field values in summary or matrix reports based on the ranges and colors we specify. To enable conditional highlighting, your report must contain at least one summary field or a custom summary formula.

The following screenshot shows where we can find the option to do conditional highlighting:

In a summary report, if we have the number, currency, or percentage columns, we have the option to conditionally highlight them with different colors, as shown in the following screenshot:

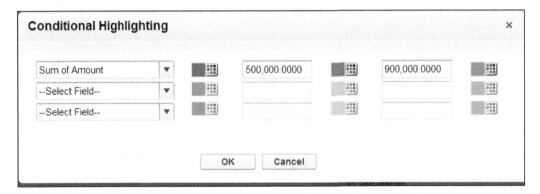

The following are the limitations/considerations of conditional highlighting:

- A maximum of three conditions per report
- Conditional highlighting can only be applied to summary rows
- Conditional highlighting is available for numerical analysis only
- The first condition is <, the second condition is <, and the third condition is >=
- Conditional highlighting is available only in matrix and summary reports

Analytic snapshots

Analytic snapshots are more like taking a picture of a report at a particular point of time and then creating a record out of it and storing it in a custom object. These records can then be used to make a report again. Users can schedule analytic snapshots to summarize data at specific times.

The benefits of using analytic snapshots include:

- Running reports faster by reporting data that is already summarized
- Creating dashboards that refresh quickly by associating them with presummarized data
- Sorting and filtering specific data summaries via list views
- Viewing trends in data via custom object records

The following diagram depicts how report data is mapped onto a custom object for further reporting. It eliminates the need to keep two different reports and compare them.

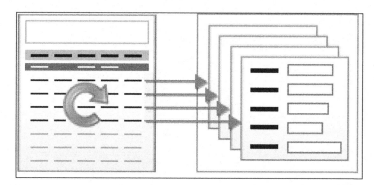

Let's create an analytic snapshot report from the demo report that we have created in the opportunity field. It will store the data every day, and then we will report the data to the custom object. Perform the following steps to generate an analytic snapshot:

1. Create a custom object named `Opportunity Report Snapshot` assuming the demo opportunity report we created at the beginning of this chapter is the source report.

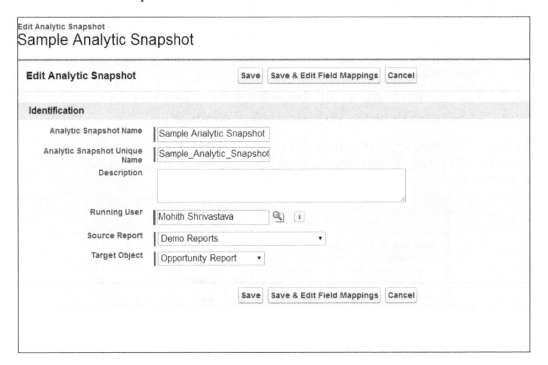

2. You will be asked to map fields between your reports and the object created.

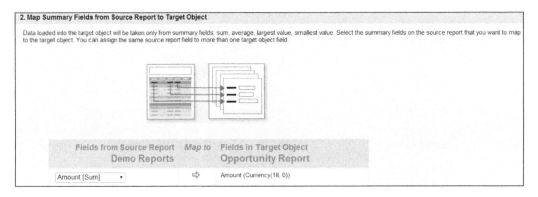

3. You can schedule when the analytic snapshot will run, as shown in the following screenshot. Then, the analytic snapshot runs at the scheduled time and dumps data into the custom object from the report. The amount of opportunities for each day will be populated. The report can't have more than 2,000 rows else the analytic snapshot will fail.

Schedule Analytic Snapshot   Save   Cancel   Unschedule Snapshot

Email Analytic Snapshot   ☑ To me ☐ To others...

Scheduled Run

	Frequency	● Daily ○ Weekly ○ Monthly	○ Every weekday ● Every day
	Start	7/4/2014 [7/4/2014]	
	End	8/4/2014 [7/4/2014]	
	Preferred Start Time	1:00 PM Show all available options...	

Exact start time will depend on job queue activity

Save   Cancel   Unschedule Snapshot

So, on a daily basis, all the data from the reports will be summarized and one can generate reporting and charting on the data aggregated in the custom objects. This feature of analytic snapshots is often used to generate a trending report.

There are certain limitations when playing with these reports; one of them is the 2,000 row limit, which spoils all the fun, but nevertheless, reporting is an effective tool in SFDC to draw analytics quickly and analyze data. For more information on analytic snapshots, refer to `https://help.salesforce.com/HTViewHelpDoc?id=data_setting_up_analytic_snap.htm&language=en_US` and understand its limitations.

Report types

Standard reporting comes out of the box with standard objects as well as custom objects, where the **Allow Reports** option is checked. Standard reports cannot be customized and automatically include standard and custom fields for each object within the report type.

Custom report types are added by an administrator in case standard report types are not enough to draw reports and one needs to relate more objects. Within a custom report type, one can specify the objects and fields that are included in the report.

 To create a custom report type, navigate to **Setup | App Setup | Create | Report Types**.

You can relate objects up to the fourth level, as shown in the following diagram. Remember to go for custom report types when standard report types don't include fields that we may need in reports.

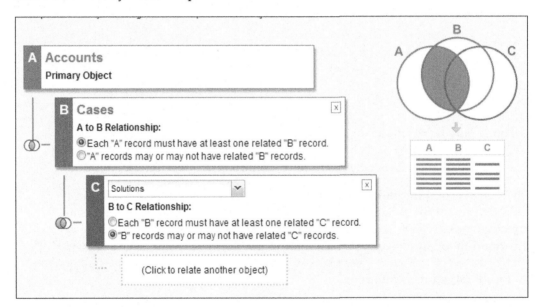

Folders

It's worthwhile to note that all reports and dashboards are stored in folders. A folder can have security features, which we will explore more in *Chapter 4, Record-level Access, Security, and Audit Features*. For reports, the folder type is Report, while for dashboards, it is Dashboard. E-mail templates are also stored in a folder type known as Email.

Summary

In this chapter, we discussed different types of reports and you learned how to convert them into dashboards. We also explored report types in depth and their need.

Salesforce has now exposed the analytics API, and that means, with the Salesforce data and analytics API, one can perform excellent reporting outside Salesforce. However, for an admin, the topics considered in this section are vital. Refer to the following links, which will definitely be valuable for you to go through:

- `http://www.salesforce.com/us/developer/docs/workbook_analytics/`
- `http://help.salesforce.com/help/pdfs/en/salesforce_dashboard_samples.pdf`
- `https://help.salesforce.com/help/pdfs/en/salesforce_reportperformance_cheatsheet.pdf`
- `https://help.salesforce.com/help/pdfs/en/salesforce_dashboards_cheatsheet.pdf`
- `https://help.salesforce.com/help/pdfs/en/salesforce_reports_enhanced_reports_tab_tipsheet.pdf`

In the next chapter, we will cover the security features provided by the Salesforce platform.

4
Record-level Access, Security, and Audit Features

Security is an important aspect of any enterprise application. The ability of a platform to provide a facility to control the access of data among various users is key to adopting the platform. The Salesforce security model is robust, and proper understanding of the security features provided by the platform can help you design a better application from the security aspect. The aim of this chapter is to explain how an administrator can configure security settings and set a security model as per the business needs. We will start by explaining **Organization-Wide Defaults** (OWD) and then explain sharing rules configuration and role hierarchy. The end of the chapter will explain audit features provided by the platform; these features can help in tracking changes that have been made in the instance.

Organization-wide sharing defaults

Before we dive deep and understand OWD in detail, it's important to recall the profile that provided us with the ability to perform **Data Manipulation Language** (**DML**) operations such as **create, read, update, and delete** (**CRUD**) access for the user. This chapter will discuss how we can control record-level access across users. OWD defines the base level security for an object across the organization. It is the default level of access as well. Let's first define the various types of OWD settings that can be configured for an object.

The following table summarizes the various values that can be set for OWD for an object:

OWD settings (for an object)	Description
Private	The records, by default, will be visible only to the owner. For a standard object, we will see that the **Grant Access Using Hierarchies** option is checked, which implies that the record will be visible to all users who are higher in the role hierarchy than the current user. We will soon define what roles are and what a hierarchy is.
Public Read Only	The record owner and users with roles hierarchically higher than the current users will have the ability to read and write the records, while other users will only have access to read the records.
Public Read/Write	The records will be editable and readable by any user.
Controlled By Parent	This is applicable for master-detail relationships. For master-detail records, we can configure this, which implies that their sharing is governed by the parent record. If the user has permission to edit the parent record, it will imply that he can also edit child records. On contact, Salesforce provides this feature to control access based on related account records.
Public Read/Write/Transfer	All users can have CRUD access and can report on the dataset. This setting is only available for cases or leads.
Full Access	All users can have CRUD access and report on all records. This setting is only available for campaigns.

Let's discuss what a role hierarchy is before we progress further. As we read in the preceding table, if the **Grant Access Using Hierarchies** checkbox is checked, then even if the **Organization-Wide Defaults** setting is set to private, the users above the role of the owner of the record still have access to edit and view the records. Hence, defining the role hierarchy for your business use case is a very important design consideration.

Consider a simple use case of a sales organization for my company named *Administrator*. The records owned by sales representatives must be accessible to the sales managers, COO, CFO, and CEO. The sales managers, CFO, and COO report to the CEO of the company, and hence, the records owned by them should still be accessible to the CEO of the company named *Administrator*.

In Salesforce, to set up this hierarchy, navigate to **Setup | Administration Setup | Manage Users | Roles**. The following screenshot shows a sample role hierarchy structure for sales organizations:

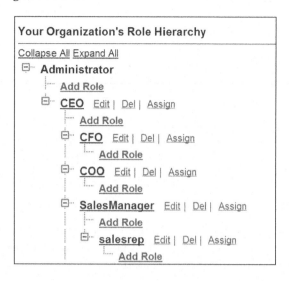

As shown in the preceding screenshot, you can use the **Add Role** button to add the necessary roles in the role hierarchy.

Role hierarchy will have meaning only if your organization has set the OWD setting as Private or Public Read Only. Public Read/Write or Full Access signifies that any user has access to edit and read records, and hence, hierarchy makes no sense here.

From the discussion so far, let's draw some conclusions that are clear at this stage:

- OWD is a base-level or default-level access, and setting this to Private will mean only owners have access to the records. Users above the record owner's role also have access to the records, provided the **Grant Access Using Hierarchies** setting is checked for objects. Again, it's important to note that for standard objects, we don't have a choice to uncheck the **Grant Access Using Hierarchies** option.

- If OWD is set to Public Read Only, it implies only record owners and users above the role hierarchy of record owners will have edit access to the records, while the rest of the users have read-only access.

- If OWD is set to Public Read/Write or Full Access, then all the users have access to edit and read the record and in the case of Full Access, even delete access to the records.

One has to navigate to **Setup | Administration Setup | Security Controls | Sharing Settings** in Salesforce to configure OWD settings for standard and custom objects; this opens the **Sharing Settings** wizard, as shown in the following screenshot:

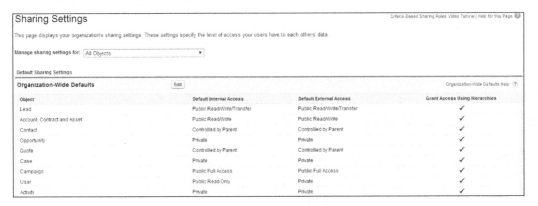

As shown in the preceding screenshot, there are two columns: **Default Internal Access** and **Default External Access**. These types of options appear when external organization-wide default settings are enabled for the organizations. Let's define these in a tabular format:

Access	Description
Default Internal Access	The internal access is for internal users and would exclude all users defined as external users.
Default External Access	External users include the following: • Authenticated website users • Chatter external users • Community users • Customer Portal users • Guest users • High-volume portal users • Partner Portal users • Service Cloud Portal users

In the older instances, when organization-wide default settings were not available, if your organization wanted Public Read Only or Public Read/Write access for internal users, but Private access for external users, one had to set the default access to Private and create a sharing rule to share records with all internal users. This method was heavier and degraded the performance of an organization with huge numbers of records.

With separate organization-wide defaults, one can set different sets of OWD for internal and external users.

Also, the **Grant Access Using Hierarchies** checkbox, which can be seen in the preceding screenshot, is editable only for custom objects. Once it is checked, the role hierarchy will be applicable for the OWD settings, as discussed earlier.

User Visibility settings

The following screenshot shows the **User Visibility Settings** window found in the **Sharing Settings** configuration page. These settings are available only in the newer instances of Salesforce.

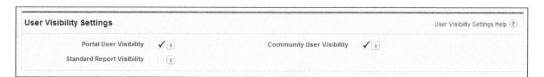

The new organization can see their **User Visibility Settings** window in the OWD section. Once these settings are checked, the users can see each other's record irrespective of the organization-wide settings. In short, the organization-wide default settings don't apply, and user-visibility settings override them, providing extra access to the users.

Profile-level Modify All and View All settings for objects

At the profile level, we have to set CRUD access. Let's recall this by observing the following screenshot:

Custom Object Permissions

	Basic Access				Data Administration	
	Read	Create	Edit	Delete	View All	Modify All
About	✓	✓	✓	✓	☐	☐
Alternative Country Names	☐	☐	☐	☐	☐	☐
Alternative State Names	☐	☐	☐	☐	☐	☐
Bank account	☐	☐	☐	☐	☐	☐
Candidates	✓	☐	☐	☐	☐	☐
Careers & Developments	✓	✓	✓	✓	☐	☐
Chatter Retention	☐	☐	☐	☐	☐	☐
Client Assignments	✓	✓	✓	✓	☐	☐
Compliance & Ethics	✓	✓	✓	✓	☐	☐
Content	✓	✓	✓	✓	☐	☐

The **Data Administration** section, as shown in the previous screenshot, has the **View All** and **Modify All** settings. If the **View All** checkbox is checked for an object, it will imply that the user will have read access to the object records, irrespective of the OWD settings. Similarly, if the **Modify All** setting is checked, the user has read and edit access of the object records, irrespective of the OWD settings we discussed so far. So, these settings are powerful, and at the profile level, one has to be very careful while checking these settings, as this will override the OWD sharing settings for the profile.

Administrative Permissions			
API Enabled	✓	Manage Letterheads	
Author Apex		Manage Mobile Configurations	
Bulk API Hard Delete		Manage Package Licenses	
Chatter Internal User	✓	Manage Public Documents	
Create and Customize List Views	✓	Manage Public List Views	
Create and Manage Communities		Manage Public Reports	
Create and Own New Chatter Groups	✓	Manage Public Templates	
Customize Application		Manage Salesforce CRM Content	
Edit HTML Templates		Manage Salesforce Knowledge	
Edit Read Only Fields		Manage Synonyms	
Invite Customers To Chatter	✓	Manage Users	
IP Restrict Requests		Moderate Chatter	
Manage Analytic Snapshots		Moderate Communities Feeds	
Manage Auth. Providers		Moderate Communities Files	
Manage Billing		Modify All Data	⇐
Manage Business Hours Holidays		Password Never Expires	
Manage Call Centers		Reset User Passwords and Unlock Users	
Manage Categories		Schedule Reports	
Manage Chatter Messages		Send Outbound Messages	✓
Manage Connections		Tag Manager	
Manage Custom Report Types		Transfer Record	
Manage Dashboards		Use Identity Features	
Manage Data Categories		Use Team Reassignment Wizards	
Manage Data Integrations		View All Data	⇐
Manage Dynamic Dashboards		View All Users	
Manage Email Client Configurations		View Data Categories	
Manage Entitlements		View Global Header	✓
Manage External Users		View Help Link	✓
Manage Knowledge Article Import/Export		View Setup and Configuration	✓

The profile has the **Modify All Data** and **View All Data** permissions under the administrative settings checked. Once these settings are checked, the sharing settings are simply ignored for all objects. So, one has to be very careful. If these settings are checked, the user gets access to all records of all objects, irrespective of the sharing settings and OWD settings.

Sharing rules and manual sharing

When the organization-wide settings are set to Private or Public Read Only, sometimes, as per business need, we will have to share the record with other users apart from the record owner and users higher in the role hierarchy. OWD sets the restrictions, and additional mechanisms open up access. To provide this access, Salesforce provides a component known as **Sharing Rules**. With sharing rules, one can share records with users who don't have access to the records. Sharing rules allocate access to users in public groups, roles, or territories. They grant users who have no access, due to the OWD settings, additional access to the records. There are various ways a record can be shared. Let's discuss all of them one by one. One can navigate to the **Sharing Settings** screen and configure sharing rules.

Record ownership-based rules

While configuring record ownership-based rules, the user will need to select which records to be shared and which users these records need to be shared with. The owner can be **Public Groups**, **Roles**, **Role and Subordinates**, and **Portal Users**. The users to share with can be **Roles**, **Roles and Subordinates**, **Public Groups**, and **Portal Users**. These options are shown in the following screenshot:

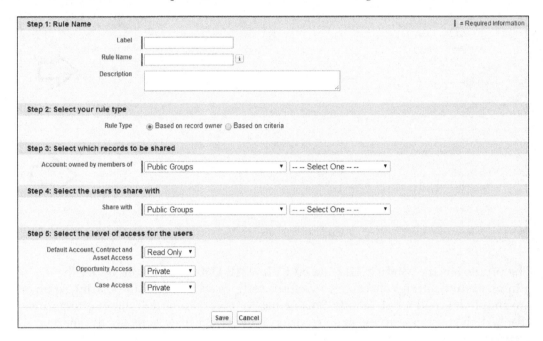

For some of the objects such as account, we have the option to provide access to the related objects in this sharing rule (case and opportunity for the account object). The access level for the records that are shared needs to be provided in the sharing rule. This will include Read Only or Read/Write access.

Let's say that you want to share records owned by sales reps among other sales reps. The rule will be very simple, as shown in the following screenshot:

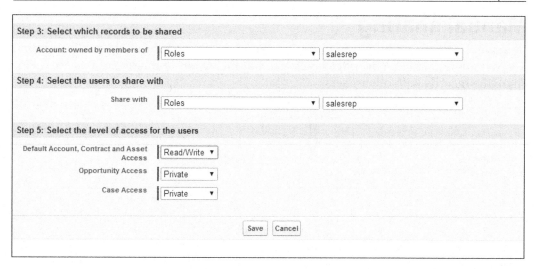

Criteria-based sharing rules

Criteria-based sharing rules allow the administrator to write rules to share records based on criteria. The criteria will be formula-based expressions (using AND or OR logic), which will use record fields. The interface to configure will look as shown in the following screenshot. The type will be criteria based instead of owner based. An example of using this type of rule can be, let's say, sharing all accounts with **Field** type as **Customer** directly with **Roles** as **salesrep**.

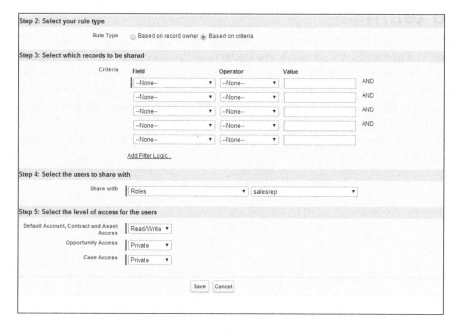

Manual sharing

In manual sharing, a **Sharing** button is provided on the record detail, and the admin keeps it intentionally on the page layout so that the owner of the record has access to share the records with other users.

Apex-based sharing

Apex-based sharing is out of the scope for an admin to develop, but an admin can request a developer to build a trigger or batch to automatically share records using a program, depending on business logic.

Account team, opportunity team, and case team

Apart from the sharing mechanisms we discussed so far, for account, we have users managing the accounts; these users are known as the account team. The account team can be given access depending on the business use case. On similar lines, for opportunity, we have the opportunity team, and for case, we have the case team to manage case collaboratively. Let's discuss all of them in detail so that you are aware of them. These are found generally on the related list of the object record. Each record (account, opportunity, or case) will have the **Add** button on the related list to add members to the team and allocate access rights to these users.

On the user's record, we have a provision to add default members (for account and opportunity only). This is shown in the following screenshot:

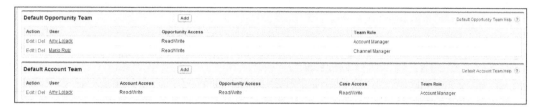

Account team members

An account team is a team of users that work together on an account. You can build an account team on each account that you own. When selecting an account team member, choose a role to indicate the role the person plays on the account. One can specify the level of access each account team member will have to the account and any contacts, opportunities, or cases associated with that account. The access range can be from read-only access to read/write.

You can also set up a default account team. Your default account team should include the users that you normally work with on your accounts. You have the option to automatically add your default account team to all of your accounts.

Opportunity team members

An opportunity team is a set of users that normally work together on sales opportunities. This team generally includes the account manager, sales representative, and sales consultant.

As an administrator, you can add opportunity team members and allocate a role for each of them (for example, *Executive Sponsor*). Also, it's vital to specify the level of access that each team member has to your opportunity. Team members might need read/write access, and others might just need read-only access. To add, edit, or delete opportunity team members, you must have read/write access on the associated opportunity. You can't use opportunity teams for private opportunities, and you can't add high-volume portal users to teams.

You can also set up a default opportunity team. Your default opportunity team should include the users that you normally work with on your opportunities. You have the option to add your default opportunity team to all of your opportunities automatically.

Case team members

A case team is a team of users who work together on a case. A case team might include a support representative, support manager, and product manager.

You need to configure a case team on the case team-related list of a case. When selecting a team member, choose a role to indicate the role the person plays on the case. Case team roles determine the level of access each case team member will have to the case. For example, you can choose a role that gives some team members read-only access and others read/write access to the case.

Audit features

In this section, we will discuss some of the audit features that an administrator must be aware of to debug and troubleshoot in case of some issues that might creep into the system. We will discuss audit log, e-mail log, Apex job, and scheduler monitoring in this section.

Audit log

Administrators should often be able to track changes made to the data objects in Salesforce during the setup phase of the environment. To facilitate this, the setup audit trail functionality is available.

Users need to navigate to **Setup | Security Controls | View Setup Audit Trails**.

In order to download the organization's full setup history for the past 180 days, click on the download link as shown in the following screenshot:

View Setup Audit Trail

The last 20 entries for your organization are listed below. You can download your organization's setup audit trail for the last six months (Excel .csv file).

View Setup Audit Trail

Date	User	Action	Section	Delegate User (?)
7/12/2014 11:18:22 AM PDT	msrivastav13@gmail.com	Created Page ParentPage	Page	
7/12/2014 11:15:42 AM PDT	msrivastav13@gmail.com	Created Page Template	Page	
7/12/2014 11:13:53 AM PDT	msrivastav13@gmail.com	Deleted Page TEST	Page	
7/12/2014 11:13:45 AM PDT	msrivastav13@gmail.com	Deleted Component TestCompoenet	Component	
7/12/2014 11:13:39 AM PDT	msrivastav13@gmail.com	Changed Page TEST	Page	
7/12/2014 11:12:37 AM PDT	msrivastav13@gmail.com	Changed Account page layout Account (Marketing) Layout	Customize Accounts	
7/12/2014 11:12:30 AM PDT	msrivastav13@gmail.com	Changed Account page layout Account Layout	Customize Accounts	
7/12/2014 11:02:55 AM PDT	msrivastav13@gmail.com	Changed Page TEST	Page	
7/12/2014 10:53:13 AM PDT	msrivastav13@gmail.com	Changed Page TEST	Page	
7/12/2014 10:52:28 AM PDT	msrivastav13@gmail.com	Changed Component TestCompoenet	Component	
7/12/2014 10:51:21 AM PDT	msrivastav13@gmail.com	Changed Page TEST	Page	
7/12/2014 10:51:16 AM PDT	msrivastav13@gmail.com	Changed Component TestCompoenet	Component	
7/12/2014 10:50:09 AM PDT	msrivastav13@gmail.com	Changed Component TestCompoenet	Component	
7/12/2014 10:49:15 AM PDT	msrivastav13@gmail.com	Changed Page TEST	Page	
7/12/2014 10:48:49 AM PDT	msrivastav13@gmail.com	Changed Page TEST	Page	
7/12/2014 10:48:03 AM PDT	msrivastav13@gmail.com	Changed Page TEST	Page	
7/12/2014 10:48:00 AM PDT	msrivastav13@gmail.com	Changed Page TEST	Page	
7/12/2014 10:47:27 AM PDT	msrivastav13@gmail.com	Changed Page TEST	Page	
7/12/2014 10:47:24 AM PDT	msrivastav13@gmail.com	Changed Page TEST	Page	
7/12/2014 10:47:21 AM PDT	msrivastav13@gmail.com	Changed Page TEST	Page	

Download setup audit trail for last six months (Excel .csv file) »

Chat

E-mail log files

E-mail logs describe all e-mails sent through Salesforce.com and can be used to help identify the status of an e-mail delivery. E-mail logs are CSV files that provide information such as the e-mail address of each e-mail sender and its recipient, the date and time each e-mail was sent, and any error code associated with each e-mail. Logs are only available for the past 30 days. The navigation path for the e-mail log is **Setup | Monitoring | Email Log Files**.

Logs contain the following data:

- The e-mail address of each e-mail sender and recipient
- The date and time each e-mail was sent
- The delivery status of each e-mail
- Any error code associated with each e-mail

You can use e-mail logs to troubleshoot encountered errors.

Batch jobs

Developers write batch jobs to process some business logic asynchronously, and also sometimes, your organization would have a batch job to clean the system (deleting some records), do territory alignment, and summarize the data. Administrators who maintain the application most of the time need to know how to monitor the batches that are running on the system. To monitor these jobs in the system, an administrator can navigate to **Setup | Monitoring | Apex Jobs**.

There will be an **Abort** link to abort any job that a system admin needs to stop.

Scheduled jobs

Scheduled jobs might be batch jobs that are scheduled by a developer using the **Schedule Apex** button on the Apex classes, page, analytic snapshot schedule, dashboard schedule, or report schedules. The administrator needs the ability to monitor these scheduled jobs and also abort or delete some of the scheduled jobs. The navigation path is **Setup | Monitoring | Scheduled Jobs**. The following screenshot shows the monitoring page:

Folder security

A folder in Salesforce is used to store reports, dashboards, documents, or e-mail templates. Folders can be public, hidden, or shared, and they can be set to read-only or read/write access. You can control the access to folder contents based on roles, permissions, public groups, and license types.

You can make a folder available to your entire organization or make it private so that only the owner has access to it. If your organization has no folder sharing enabled, then the sharing options are not so granular, and the following screenshot confirms the options that are available. It also shows the **Folder Sharing** setting to control folder visibility for reports and dashboards. The navigation path for the folder is **Setup | Customize | Reports & Dashboards | Folder Sharing**.

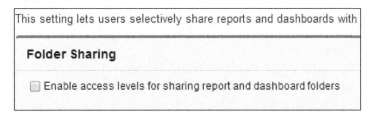

The following screenshot shows the folder visibility settings that the administrator can configure:

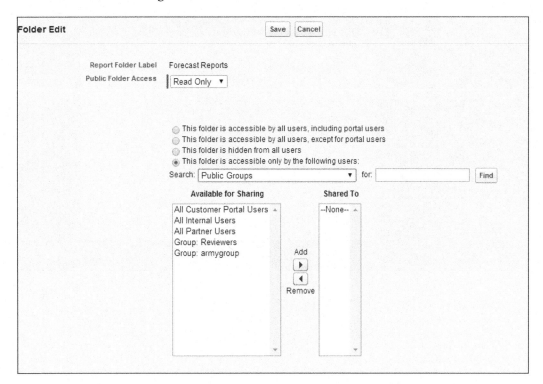

If folder sharing is enabled, then the sharing options of a folder can be more granular. As shown in the following screenshot, once we click on the share link for the folder, we can set access for roles, roles and subordinates, users, portal roles, and groups. The access levels are **Viewer**, **Editor**, and **Manager**. Let's define these access levels:

- **Viewer access to report and dashboard folders**: This access allows level users to only see the reports and dashboards, but one can't edit them. Some users might have administrative user permissions that give them greater access.

- **Editor access to report and dashboard folders**: This access level allows users to edit the reports and dashboards. Editor permission also allows them to move the reports from one folder to an other.

- **Manager access to report and dashboard folders**: This access level provides the ability to view, edit, and also manage other users' access to folders, change their properties, or delete them.

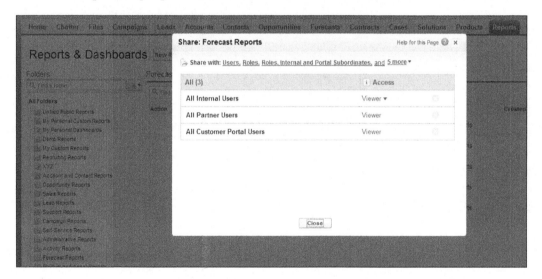

It's important to know that certain administrative permissions are necessary to allow editor and manager access to the folders. These are listed in the following table:

User permission	Description
Create and Customize Dashboards	This allows us to create, edit, and delete dashboards in the `Personal Dashboard` folder. If a folder is shared, then a user, depending on their access rights, can create dashboards.
Create and Customize Reports	This allows us to create reports in the `Personal Report` folder.
Create Dashboard Folders	This allows us to create dashboard folders and manage them if sharing rights allow.
Create Report Folders	This allows us to create report folders and manage them if sharing rights permit.
Edit My Dashboards	This allows us to edit, transfer, and delete dashboards that you created in shared folders.
Edit My Reports	This allows us to edit, transfer, and delete reports that you created in shared folders.
Manage Dashboards in Public Folders	This allows us to create, edit, delete dashboards, and manage their sharing in all public dashboard folders, which does not include others' personal folders. This permission allows users to edit and share dashboards in all folders, including hidden folders. They also get this permission for the following: • Create and customize dashboards • Create dashboard folders • Edit my dashboards • View dashboards in public folders To edit a dynamic dashboard, users also need the Manage Dynamic Dashboards and View My Team's Dashboards permissions.
Manage Reports in Public Folders	This allows us to create, edit, and delete reports, and manage their sharing in all public report folders, which does not include others' personal folders. This permission allows users to edit and share reports in all folders, including hidden folders. They also get permission for the following: • Create and Customize Reports • Create Report Folders • Edit My Reports • View Reports in Public Folders

User permission	Description
View Dashboards in Public Folders	This allows us to view dashboards in public dashboard folders.
View Reports in Public Folders	This allows us to view reports in public report folders.

Summary

This chapter presented record-level access security provided by the Salesforce platform. We restricted ourselves to not dig deeper into territory management at this point, and for organizations that don't have territory management enabled, this chapter will be enough to troubleshoot problems around record-level access. We covered folder sharing in detail, and this should help us manage security around report and dashboard sharing. There are some more modules such as content, knowledge, and ideas that follow a specific security model, and *Chapter 7, An Overview of Sales and Service Cloud*, should give an idea of how to manage security around the same. This chapter is vital as it covers record-level access, and most of the time, administration is about records' visibility for users.

The next chapter will cover the best practices for data loading, and we will explore the data loader tool. We will also explore session management in the following chapter.

5
Session Management, Data Loader, and Data Loading Best Practices

In this chapter, we will explore the best practices for session management in Salesforce. We will explore the password policy, session settings, and session management in detail. Data loading is an important activity, and there are certain tools a Salesforce administrator must be aware of to make life easier. We will also have a section that will help us through the fundamental best practices that one must be aware of while loading data.

Password policies

The password policy for an organization is an essential component to enforce users to follow the best practices to set passwords.

The navigation path to set the password policy for the admin is **Setup | Security Controls | Password Policies**.

The settings that can be configured in relation to the password policy are as follows:

- The expiry date of the password (default is 90 days). Keep this optimal so that users are enforced to change the password frequently to avoid hacking.

- Enforcing password history. This is important to prevent users from repeating the same password every time.

- The minimum length of the password and its complexity.

- The number of invalid attempts that the system can allow before locking the user.

- The effective locking period and also a checkbox to obscure the secret answer to reset the password.

The following screenshot shows the **Password Policies** settings page for an administrator; one can configure the previously mentioned parameters here:

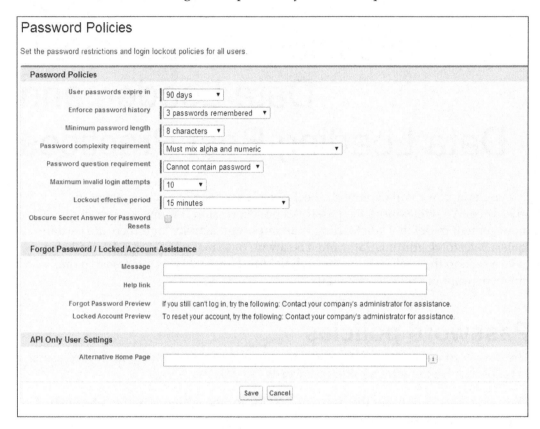

Session settings

Session settings are needed to protect the customer data from getting hacked. Imagine that your session timeout time is 2 hours; this implies that once an attacker obtains the session ID or once a session ID is generated, the session ID will remain active for 2 hours. It's advisable to set the timeout time value as low as possible.

The following screenshot shows the **Session Settings** page, where an administrator can configure the **Timeout value** under **Session Timeout** for his application users:

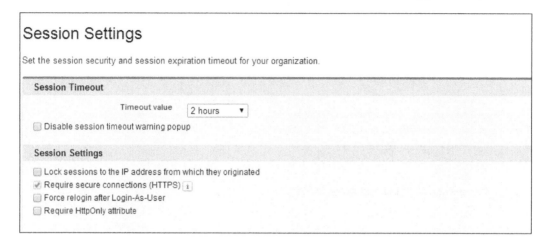

If you have logged in to Salesforce, sometimes you would have observed that we don't need to retype the complete login credentials; this feature can be disabled as a security measure.

The following screenshot shows the **Caching** and **Autocomplete** login configurations for the application. Some organizations prefer SMS-based authentication, and one can enable this as shown in the screenshot. Sometimes, there is a risk of pages getting iFramed to other websites. This is technically called as **clickjacking**. In order to prevent clickjacking, Salesforce provides options to protect the setup, non-setup, and Visualforce pages (pages custom built by the developer) against clickjacking.

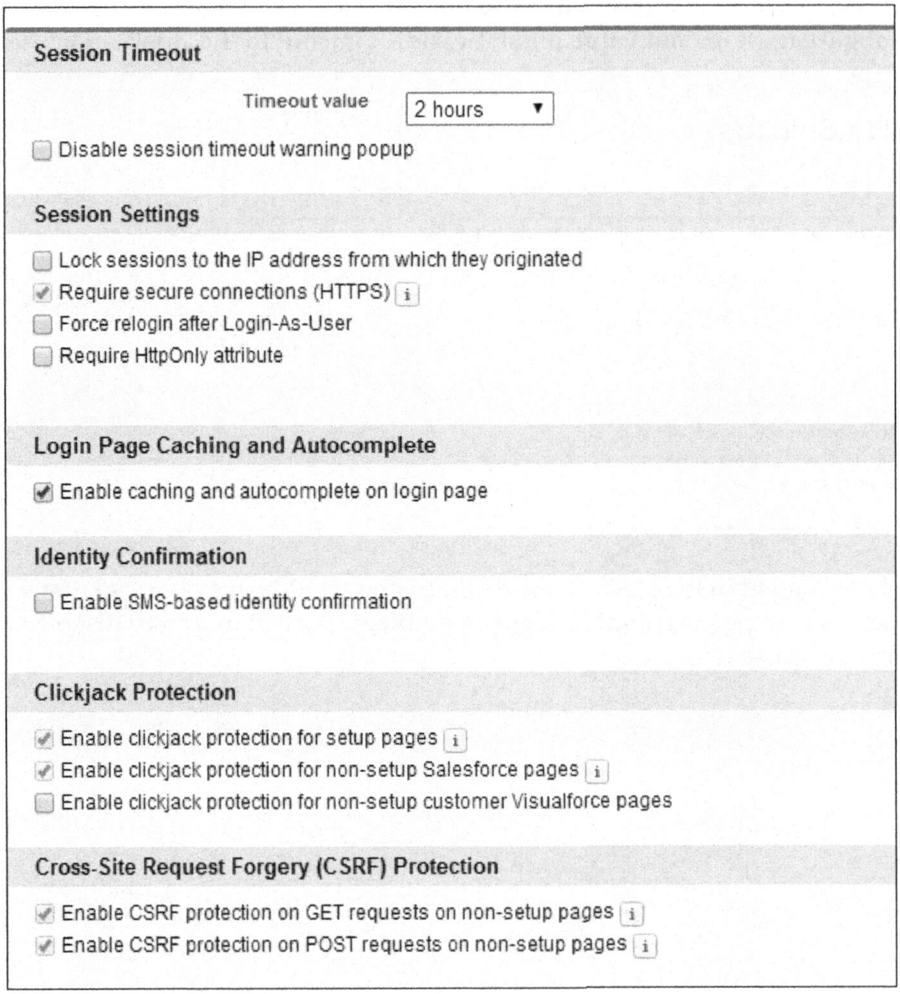

Session Timeout

Timeout value   2 hours ▼

☐ Disable session timeout warning popup

Session Settings

☐ Lock sessions to the IP address from which they originated
☑ Require secure connections (HTTPS) ⓘ
☐ Force relogin after Login-As-User
☐ Require HttpOnly attribute

Login Page Caching and Autocomplete

☑ Enable caching and autocomplete on login page

Identity Confirmation

☐ Enable SMS-based identity confirmation

Clickjack Protection

☑ Enable clickjack protection for setup pages ⓘ
☑ Enable clickjack protection for non-setup Salesforce pages ⓘ
☐ Enable clickjack protection for non-setup customer Visualforce pages

Cross-Site Request Forgery (CSRF) Protection

☑ Enable CSRF protection on GET requests on non-setup pages ⓘ
☑ Enable CSRF protection on POST requests on non-setup pages ⓘ

In **Cross-Site Request Forgery (CSRF)**, an attacker uses the cookie of the browser to obtain session information and then performs a malicious attack on the website. The administrators can prevent non-setup pages from this attack, as shown in the preceding screenshot.

Session management

Session management is a new feature in Salesforce to view and abort active sessions. The navigation path for the session management window is **Setup | Security Controls | Session Management**.

The following screenshot shows how the information is listed. One can click on the **Remove** button to abort active sessions, and then users will need to log in to that application again.

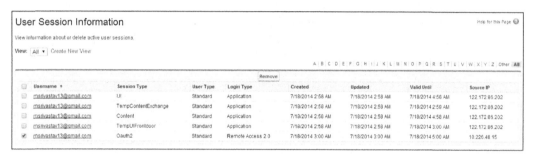

Data loader

IT applications are meant to make our life simple. In order to load data from a CSV file on a computer to Salesforce, we have a native built-in tool provided by Salesforce; this is known as the data loader. To download data loader from your organization, navigate to **Setup | Data Management | Data Loader**; on this page, you will see the **Download the Data Loader** link to download the tool to your local device. Once the tool is downloaded, we can install it. The tool can work on both Windows and Mac machine systems.

The following screenshot shows the link to download the data loader once you navigate to the **Data Loader Setup** page; it also shows the data loader UI. One can export data from Salesforce, insert data into a Salesforce table, update data on Salesforce, or delete the data.

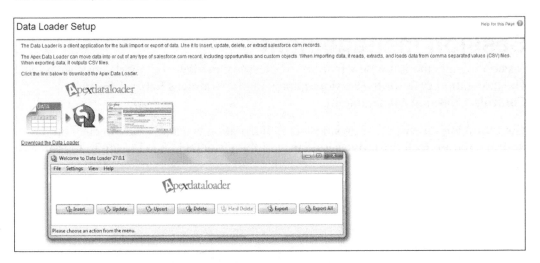

An important step in data migration is to first connect this data loader to your organization. Salesforce data insertion can be in your production organization or in a sandbox. Sandbox is a testing environment where all code is built and data is validated by application users, and production is the live environment where end users use the built applications.

The following are the steps that need to be followed to connect the data loader to the SFDC system:

1. On top of the data loader UI screen, we have the **Settings** option. This is where we set some key parameters such as credentials and select whether we need to connect to a sandbox or production instance.

   The following screenshot shows the screen generated in the data loader for the **Settings** option. For sandbox, the server host will be test.salesforce.com, while for production, it is login.salesforce.com. If your organization uses proxy, then you will need to configure the proxy settings as well. The **Time Zone** field is important because all the date and time fields that we load from Excel will be considered by default based on the time zone we set. It's a little tricky to understand mapping of date and time fields from Excel; by default, it takes the computer time and also the time zone specified in the data loader settings. If the wrong time zone is specified, the data loader uses GMT time.

Batch size:	200
Insert null values:	☐
Assignment rule:	
Server host (clear for default):	https://login.salesforce.com
Reset URL on Login (clear to turn off):	☑
Compression (check to turn off):	☐
Timeout (in seconds):	540
Query request size:	500
Generate status files for exports:	☐
Read all CSVs with UTF-8 encoding:	☐
Write all CSVs with UTF-8 encoding:	☐
Use European date format (dd/mm/yyyy)	☐
Allow field truncation:	☐
Use Bulk API:	☐
Enable serial mode for Bulk API:	☐
Upload Bulk API Batch as Zip File (enable to upload binary attachments):	☐
Time Zone:	America/Los_Angeles
Proxy host:	
Proxy port:	
Proxy username:	
Proxy password:	
Proxy NTLM domain:	

The last batch finished at 38. Use 38 to continue from your last location.

Start at row:	0

2. For the **Insert**, **Update**, and **Upsert** options, one has to do mapping from an Excel file (the `.csv` file). The **Upsert** option uses external IDs. The data, if not found in the SFDC database, will be updated; otherwise, a fresh entry of the record is created in Salesforce.

3. For data extraction, use the **Export** option. The **Export** option will retrieve data from the Salesforce database into a CSV file (use Excel or Notepad++ to view this file). The following screenshot shows how to browse to the desktop file and select the SFDC object for data loading:

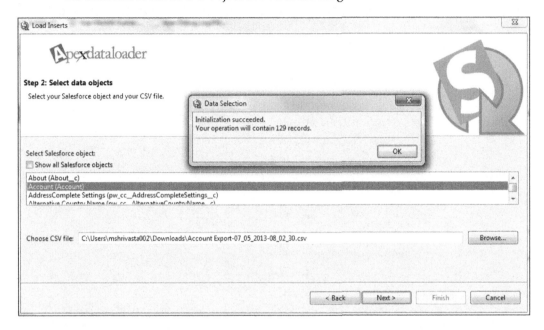

4. An important stage while using the data loader is field mapping; the following screenshot shows the **Mapping Dialog** window. There is an auto-match option that can be handy as well, as it can automatically map fields between the CSV and SFDC object fields.

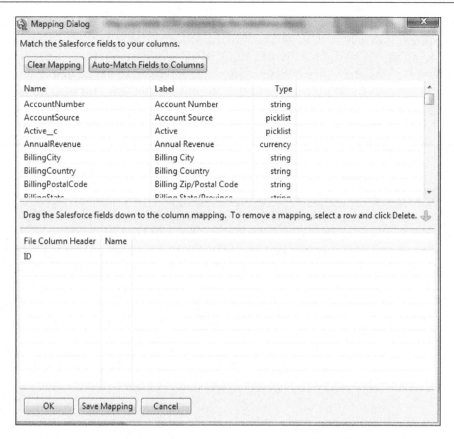

Importance of VLOOKUP and external IDs

When we are loading data from an external legacy application, most of the time we have master-detail (parent-child) relationships where, after we load the parent data, we get parent IDs and then use this parent ID to load the child data. Now, imagine that we have a Salesforce instance called system A; it has accounts and contacts data, and we need to load all the data into another Salesforce instance called system B. To link the contacts to the account, we need an account ID stamped on the **Contact Account** field. We can get an account ID only when we load accounts. An external ID helps here to load this data into system B. We can directly use the parent's external ID to map all child records and do an upsert of the child record via the master's external ID.

There is another way in case you have no external ID (most likely if the data is not loaded from an external system and we are transferring data from one Salesforce instance to another). To do this, Excel's VLOOKUP is our friend. It's worth spending some time via YouTube to learn this technique. It is related to Excel. In short, you will need to maintain one more column in your old account file and map all old IDs to the newly generated ones. Once you have done this, use the column to do a VLOOKUP for all account IDs of the contact file to the newly generated account IDs, and then one can load data to establish association.

Summary

This chapter covered session management and data loading techniques and tips. It also showed us how to use the data loader tool for data loading. In the next chapter, we will see some of the common challenges that an admin might encounter in their day-to-day activities and how one can tackle these using troubleshooting techniques.

6

Troubleshooting Common Problems

In this chapter, we will look at some common problems that one might face as a new admin to the Salesforce.com software or Force.com platform, and we will document how to approach troubleshooting, step by step. Most of the problems I will discuss here are ones that I encountered in my real-time projects. The most crucial aspect of any debugging is how we approach the problem and follow the right path without getting misguided. As concepts such as profiles, security, and roles are covered, we are now all set to combine whatever we learned so far to utilize to the maximum.

Problem statement 1

One of your users raises a concern that, in spite of entering the right password, they are not able to access Salesforce.com. As an administrator, your challenge is to figure out the root cause.

Debugging steps

The following are the steps to debug the problem:

1. Salesforce sometimes performs system upgrade and maintenance. Due to this, there can be instances when Salesforce won't be available. So, first ensure that the problem is not due to the maintenance window time. One can visit the Salesforce trust (`https://trust.salesforce.com/trust/status/`) website for the current status of their instance name. The instance name can be obtained from your SFDC URL (NA11, NA0, and so on).

   The following screenshot shows how the information is shown on the trust website:

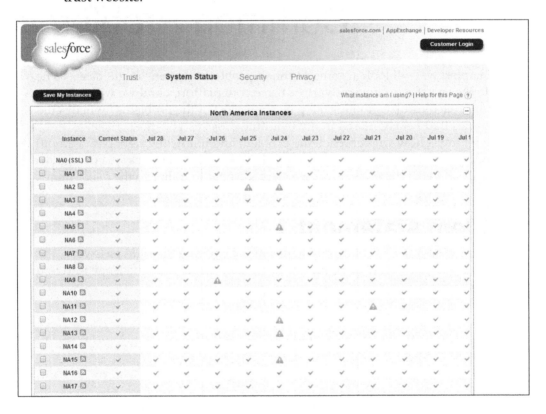

2. If this is not the problem, then one can navigate to the user (**Manage User | Users**) and see the login history on the user record. The error is clearly printed, and with this, you will be able to help your users access the Salesforce system again. The following screenshot shows how the login history-related list can help us debug login issues:

Login History							Login History Help ?
Login Time	Source IP	Login Type	Status		Application	Login URL	Community
8/26/2014 10:41:57 AM PDT	122.171.96.116	Application	Success		Browser	ap1.salesforce.com	
8/26/2014 10:41:37 AM PDT	122.171.96.116	Application	Failed: Computer activation required		Browser	login.salesforce.com	
8/24/2014 11:45:04 PM PDT	54.167.109.22	Other Apex API	Success		N/A		
8/24/2014 11:45:02 PM PDT	54.167.109.22	Other Apex API	Success		N/A		
8/23/2014 12:58:41 PM PDT	Salesforce.com IP	Remote Access 2.0	Success	**Invalid Password**	Salesforce Developers	login.salesforce.com	
8/23/2014 12:58:33 PM PDT	122.172.84.71	Remote Access Client	Success		Browser	login.salesforce.com	
8/23/2014 3:15:36 AM PDT	Salesforce.com IP	Remote Access 2.0	Success		Salesforce Developers	login.salesforce.com	
8/23/2014 3:15:29 AM PDT	122.172.84.71	Remote Access Client	Success		Browser	login.salesforce.com	
8/23/2014 2:20:07 AM PDT	122.172.84.71	Application	Invalid Password		Browser	gs0.salesforce.com	
8/23/2014 2:18:19 AM PDT	122.172.84.71	Application	Success		Browser	gs0.salesforce.com	

Download login history for last six months, including logins from outside the website, such as API logins (Excel .csv file) »

Problem statement 2

An object's organization-wide default setting is set as private, but still, one of your users is able to access the record. As an administrator, your challenge is to find out how the user is granted access.

Debugging steps

The following are the steps to debug the problem:

1. The first step is to check the profile of the user and find out whether the profile has the **Modify All** or **View All** settings checked at the global level (administrative privileges) or at the object level. If yes, then this is causing the issue, and it might be worth putting the user under a different profile or creating a new profile and assigning the user to the new one. Also, one has to be judicious enough to conclude whether removing these permissions from the profile will impact other users.

2. If it is not a profile issue, we need to look at whether the user has a permission set assigned and whether the permission set grants access through the **Modify All** and **View All** settings. If yes, then modify the permission set.

3. Sharing rules can be the culprit as well. It is important to spend time and find out if sharing rules exist that are granting view/edit access to the user.

4. If the **Grant Access using Hierarchies** checkbox is checked, then consider the role of the user and the record owner, and compare and figure out whether the user is above the record owner role hierarchy.

5. Check the manual sharing settings using the **Sharing** button on the record details page. It might be that someone shared the record with other users manually.

Problem statement 3

As an administrator, you added the field on the page layout, but still, your users can't see the field.

Debugging steps

This problem is primarily due to field-level security. The visibility of your field is set to false, and this has caused the issue. When field-level security is not visible, adding the field on the page layout will still keep the field invisible.

Problem statement 4

You are using a data loader or Informatica Cloud (a Cloud-based tool to load data into Salesforce from a legacy system), and you don't see a field for mapping.

Debugging steps

This is primarily due to field-level security. The visibility of your field is set to false, and this has caused the issue. When field-level security is not visible, adding the field on the page layout will still keep the field invisible.

Problem statement 5

As an administrator, you have been asked to debug time-based workflows. They are not firing as expected. The challenge in front of you is to debug and figure out the root cause of the issue.

Debugging steps

The following steps will help debug this problem:

1. The first check is to repeat the same transaction (the same workflow) on the record in a sandbox instance to satisfy the criteria of the time-based workflow. Observe the criteria, as the records might not be satisfying the workflow criteria.

2. Monitor the time-based workflow queue. The navigation path is **Setup | Monitoring | Time-Based Workflow**.

3. You can reduce the time frame temporarily for an hour to observe the results to figure out whether the time-based rule is firing.

4. The last resort will be asking your developer to look at the debug logs to find out whether the time-based rule is triggering.

The following screenshot shows the time-based workflow monitoring queue:

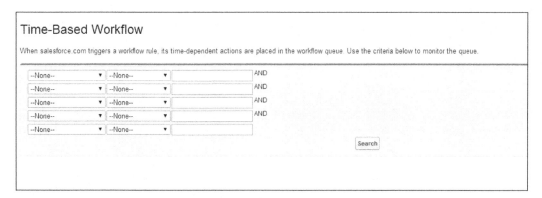

Problem statement 6

As an administrator, you have been asked to install an app from AppExchange. The challenge is to search for the application in AppExchange and perform the installation.

Debugging steps

The following steps will help debug this problem:

1. Navigate to `https://appexchange.salesforce.com/`.

2. Search for your application, for example, the Salesforce Milestones PM application that's distributed by Salesforce Labs. Salesforce Labs provides many apps for free, and it's worth trying these applications.

3. The following screenshot shows the Milestone PM app that we searched for. By clicking on the **Get it Now** button and logging in to your instance with your credentials, you will be able to install these applications.

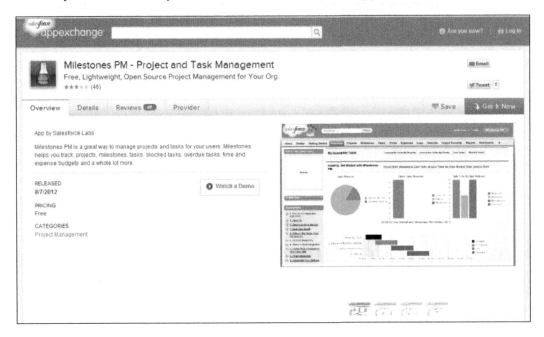

4. After installation, one can find the application in the installed packages list. The installed packages can be found by navigating to **Setup | Installed Packages**.

    The following screenshot shows the list of installed packages in my instance:

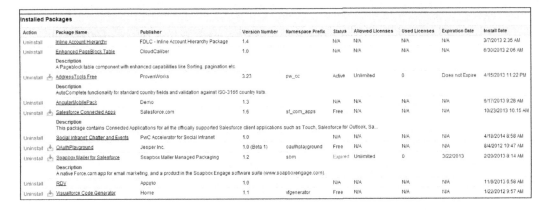

Note that it's always good to be aware of applications that are present on AppExchange. Some of them are free, while the rest might cost a little, but these provide excellent and quick solutions to your business needs.

Problem statement 7

You want your workflow to fire once more after a field value is updated via workflows. However, for some reason, the workflow is not triggering.

Debugging steps

Remember that workflows don't have any order of execution. One can't ensure that they follow a specific order. Salesforce provides a checkbox for the field updates to re-evaluate the workflows after the fields are updated.

The following screenshot shows the settings on the field updates that, as an administrator, one needs to apply to ensure that workflow rules are triggered again:

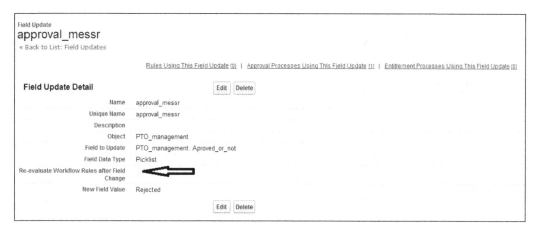

Problem statement 8

As an administrator, you have been assigned a task to assign different page layouts for an object for different record types based on the profile. Your challenge is to navigate to a place where this matrix can be configured for profile and record types. Let's assume that we have an object named *Job Applications*, with two different page layouts and two different record types (electronics and mechanical).

Debugging steps

It is vital not to go to each profile and configure the layout. On the **Page Layouts** page of an object, SFDC provides an option to do page layout assignment. By clicking on the assignment, one can assign different layouts based on the profile for each record type. The following screenshot shows the page where an administrator can configure these layouts:

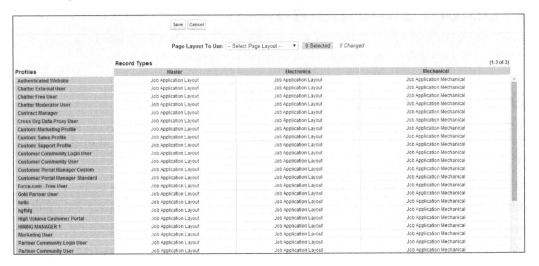

Problem statement 9

Your developer has developed a Visualforce page, and some of your users, whom you are accessing, are raising a concern that they have been getting insufficient privileges when trying to access the Visualforce page.

Debugging steps

This is a very common issue where a developer forgets to assign profiles that need access to the Visualforce page. As an administrator, one can easily solve this by assigning profiles to the Visualforce security settings.

To do this, navigate to the Visualforce page (**Setup** | **Develop** | **Pages**).

As shown in the following screenshot, one can click on the **Security** link on the Visualforce page:

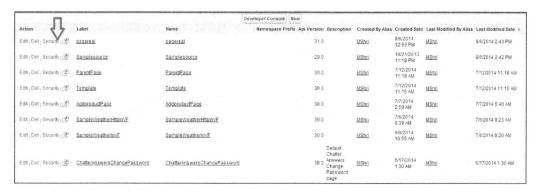

Now, when you click on the **Security** link as shown in the preceding screenshot, you can assign appropriate profiles to the Visualforce page. The following screenshot shows how one can assign the available profiles to enable them in order to provide access to various profiles:

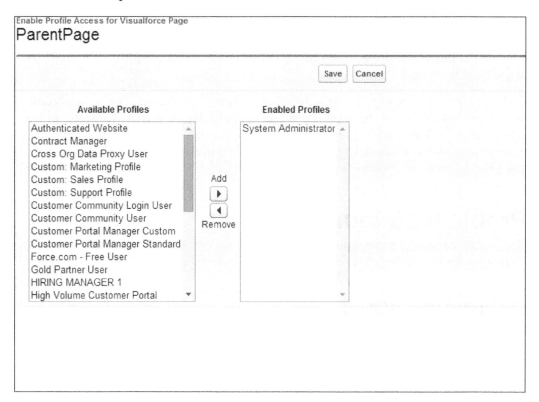

There are also security settings for Apex classes. Apex classes are written to solve business problems using the Apex language. This requires developer skills, but as an administrator, you can take care of the security of these classes based on the profile. Sometimes, users might not be able to perform some business operations as they don't have the permission to access the Apex class that's performing this business operation.

Problem statement 10

The challenge is to debug an approval process, and for some reason, the process has stopped working or you have been asked to enhance it further. You are a new administrator to the firm, and you have no prior knowledge of what's already built and how to analyze the existing approval flow.

Debugging steps

The first step would be to take a print of the approval flow diagram. You will find this on the approval process. The **View Diagram** button on the approval process will display the flowchart.

Understand the business need for which this process was written. This is important as you will get a sense of the actions written. Go to each of the approval steps and actions, and work on each criteria and action; use the Salesforce debug log to get more information on what's triggering and what's not. An obvious reason could be some logical issue on criteria or actions.

Problem statement 11

The profile settings are configured to restrict functionality, but still, the users are getting access to functionality. You have been asked to debug this behavior.

Debugging steps

The following steps will help debug this problem:

1. Double-check the profile settings for the profile that has been restricted.
2. Go to the user's page and see if the user has a permission set assigned. The permission set provides extra access and overrides profile restrictions.

Problem statement 12

You added a field on the page layout as read-only, but still, an administrator is able to edit the same.

Debugging steps

There is no need to worry as this is the expected behavior. An administrator can edit fields even if the field is read-only at page layout. This applies to all the different profiles other than system administrator.

Summary

This chapter covered most of the common challenges an administrator might encounter. The debugging steps provide a guide and path to approach the solution. Salesforce has a great community, and you can always browse through https://success.salesforce.com/, http://developer.salesforce.com, or my favorite community for Q&A related to Salesforce problems at http://salesforce.stackexchange.com/. Our next chapter will explain sales and service cloud features provided by Salesforce.com to manage the sales and support cycle. Salesforce has evolved as a maturity model, and we will discuss this in the following chapter.

7
An Overview of Sales and Service Cloud

Salesforce can be classified as a **Software as a Service (SaaS)** or a cloud software, and was originally built around CRM capabilities. Over the years, new functionalities have been added, and the platform functionalities (**Platform as a Service (PaaS)**) have been made generally available, making it possible to build a variety of custom applications in the cloud.

In this chapter, we will take a look at the sales cycle and some of the sales cloud modules that Salesforce provides out of the box. Salesforce.com can also be deployed for case management and product servicing. Salesforce.com service cloud applications are increasingly being used globally, and they provide a huge set of out-of-the-box features such as entitlements, knowledge management, content management, live agent, milestones, ideas, communities, and many more. Most of them require a feature license and many are provided out of the box. In this chapter, we will devote our time to getting a brief overview of service cloud features provided by the platform. At the end of this chapter, we will devote some time to exploring Salesforce as a maturity model and discuss which part of the sales cycle Salesforce will fit in. Each of the topics explained in this chapter can be a chapter in itself, and hence, this chapter will just brief you on each topic. To understand and dig deeper, you can dive into the Salesforce guides that come with each of the modules, after you have acquired a basic understanding of Salesforce. For example, territory management itself is so vast; in order to learn how to configure and use it, Salesforce provides a guide *Deploying Territory Management* that can be read. My aim in this chapter will be to introduce these modules and their business use cases so that the reader is aware of the modules provided by Salesforce for sales and service cloud applications.

A sales cycle

A typical sales cycle starts from a campaign. An example of a campaign can be a conference or a seminar where marketing individuals explain the product offering of the company to their prospects. Salesforce provides a campaign object to store this data. A campaign may involve different processes, and the campaign management module of Salesforce is simple. A matured campaign management system will have features such as sending e-mails to campaign members in bulk, and tracking how many people really opened and viewed the e-mails, and how many of them responded to the e-mails. Some of these processes can be custom built in Salesforce, but out of the box, Salesforce has a campaign member object apart from the campaign where members are selected by marketing reps. Members can be leads or contacts of Salesforce. A campaign generates leads. Leads are the prospects that have shown interest in the products and offerings of the company.

The **lead management** module provides a lead object to store all the leads in the system. These prospects are converted into accounts, contacts, and opportunities when the prospect qualifies as an account. Salesforce provides a **Lead Convert** button to convert these leads into accounts, contacts, and opportunities. Features such as Web-to-Lead provided by the platform are ideal for capturing leads in Salesforce.

Accounts can be B2B (business to business) or B2C (business to consumer). B2C in Salesforce is represented as person accounts. This is a special feature that needs to be enabled by a request from Salesforce. It's a record type where person accounts fields are from contacts.

Contacts are people, and they are stored in objects in the contact object. They have a relationship with accounts (a relationship can be both master-detail as well as lookup.)

An opportunity generates revenue if its status is closed won. Salesforce provides an object known as opportunities to store a business opportunity. The sales reps typically work on these opportunities, and their job is to close these deals and generate revenue. Opportunities have a stage field and stages start from prospecting to closed won or closed lost.

Opportunity management provided by Salesforce consists of objects such as opportunity line items, products, price books, and price book entries.

Products in Salesforce are the objects that are used as a lookup to junction objects such as an opportunity line item. An opportunity line item is a junction between an opportunity and a line item.

Price books are price listings for products in Salesforce. A product can have a standard or custom price book. Custom price books are helpful when your company is offering products at discounts or varied prices for different customers based on market segmentation.

Salesforce also provides a **quote management** module that consists of a quote object and quote line items that sales reps can use to send quotes to customers.

The **Order management** module is new to the Salesforce CRM, and Salesforce provides an object known as orders that can generate an order from the draft state to the active state on accounts and contracts. Most companies use an ERP such as a SAP system to do order management. However, now, Salesforce has introduced this new feature, so on closed opportunities from accounts, you can create orders.

The following screenshot explains the sales process and the sales life cycle from campaign to opportunity management:

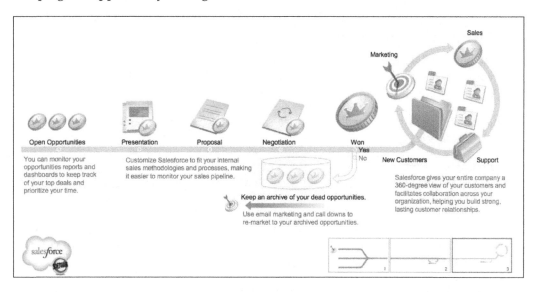

As already discussed, this chapter will provide just an overview. The sales process and modules such as lead management, opportunity management, or account management can themselves be chapters, and are out of the scope of this book. To read more, I would recommend that you go through the Salesforce documentation available at `http://www.salesforce.com/ap/assets/pdf/cloudforce/ SalesCloud-TheSalesCloud.pdf`.

Territory management

This feature is very helpful for organizations that run sales processes by sales territories. Let's say you have an account and your organization has a private sharing model. The account has to be worked on by sales representatives of the eastern as well as western regions. Presently, the owner is the sales rep of the eastern region, and because of the private sharing model, the sales rep of the western region will not have access. We could have used sharing rules to provide access, but the challenge is also to do a forecasting of the revenue generated from opportunities for both reps, and this is where writing sharing rules simply won't help us. We need the territory management feature of Salesforce for this, where you can retain opportunities and transfer representatives across territories, draw reports based on territories, and share accounts across territories extending the private sharing model. The key feature of this module is that it works with customizable forecasting only. We will shortly describe customizable forecasting in the next sections when we look at forecasting in detail.

Basic configurations

We will explore the basic configuration needed to set up territory management. This feature is not enabled in your instance by default. To enable it, you have to log a case with Salesforce and explain its need.

The basic navigation path for the territories feature is **Setup | Manage Users | Manage Territories**.

Under **Manage Territories**, we have the settings to set the default access level for accounts, contacts, opportunities, and cases. This implies that when a new territory is created, the access level will be based on the default settings configured.

There is a checkbox named **Forecast managers can manage territories**. Once checked, forecast managers can add accounts to territories, manage account assignment rules, and manage users.

Under **Manage Territories | Settings**, you can see two different buttons, which are as follows:

- **Enable Territory Management**: This button forecasts hierarchy, and data is copied to the territory hierarchy. Each forecast hierarchy role will have a territory automatically created.

- **Enable Territory Management from Scratch**: This is for new organizations. On clicking this button, the forecast data is wiped, and please note that this is irreversible.

Based on the role of the user, a territory is automatically assigned to the user. On the **Territory Details** page, one can use **Add Users** to assign users to territories.

Account assignment rules

To write account assignment rules, navigate to **Manage Territories | Hierarchy**. Select a territory and click on **Manage Rules** in the list related to the account assignment rules.

Enter the rule name and define the filter criteria based on the account field. You can apply these rules to child territories if you check the **Apply to Child Territories** checkbox.

> There is a lot more to explore on this topic, but that's beyond the scope of this book. To explore more, I would recommend that you read the documentation from Salesforce available at https://na9.salesforce.com/help/pdfs/en/salesforce_territories_implementation_guide.pdf.

Forecasting

Forecasting helps to provide an estimate of the possible revenue for a time period. Forecasting can be done using custom-defined fiscal quarters or a standard fiscal year. It rolls up the amounts from opportunities. A forecast can be on opportunities, product families, and also on opportunity splits. With Salesforce.com, two different types of forecasting are possible:

- Customizable forecasting
- Collaborative forecasting

Customizable forecasting

As the name suggests, customizable forecasting allows forecasting as per custom-defined quarters. Let's see how we can enable customizable forecasting in our Salesforce instance. To enable this feature, you will need to navigate to **Customize | Forecasts (Customizable) | Forecasts Hierarchy | Enable Customizable Forecasting**.

The following screenshot shows the options to configure forecast settings once the forecast feature is enabled:

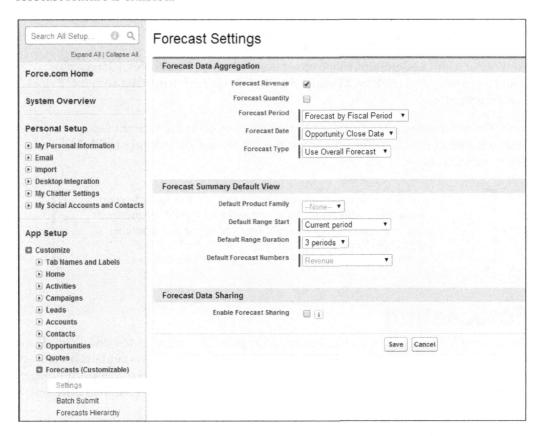

The **Forecast Data Aggregation** section will define the date range for which the forecasting report will be formed, and the type of forecast (overall or only product-based; overall is used when organizations don't have products). The **Enable Forecast Sharing** checkbox allows forecasts to be shared with other users. Most of the options in the screenshot are self-explanatory, but for more information, refer to the documentation available at `https://help.salesforce.com/htviewhel pdoc?err=1&id=customize_forecastsettings.htm&siteLang=en_US`.

The following screenshot shows how to mass-submit users, so that for all those users, the forecast history is calculated and also the data becomes available to the users:

The forecast hierarchy is automatically formed from the role hierarchy when customizable hierarchy is enabled. The following screenshot shows the **Forecast Hierarchy** window; to add users, you will need to click on **Enable Users**, and also, there is an **Edit Manager** link to add forecast managers. Forecast managers can add adjustments to the forecasts of their subordinates.

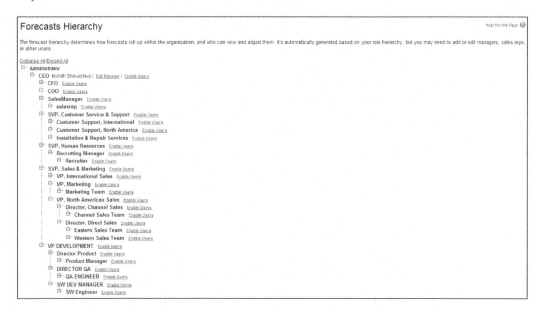

Let's now take a look at the **Forecasts** tab. It's different from other tabs. It is more like a report that shows forecasts of individuals, and it provides an option to select the forecast for a specific individual. It automatically shows the forecast based on opportunities, and one has the option to override and submit the new forecast. On submitting, a forecast history is formed, and data is also made available for reporting. The forecast can also be overridden by forecast managers, and the forecast calculation is automatically adjusted.

The following screenshot shows how the forecast screen will look once the **Forecasts** tab is clicked. Please note that the arrows on the screenshot explain what each button does.

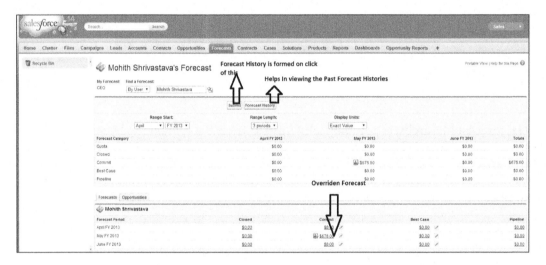

In the preceding screenshot, you can see that the forecast categories include **Closed**, **Commit**, **Best Case**, and **Pipeline**. It's important at this point that we define these categories. The following diagram best explains them. As you can see, forecasting categories are cumulative.

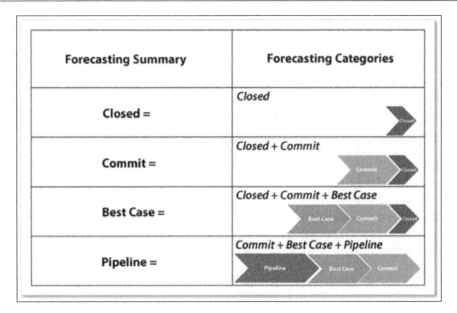

As shown in the following screenshot, the opportunity stage field controls the mapping to the forecast category:

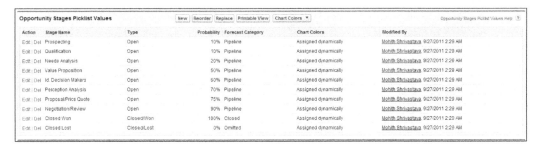

Also, note that the **Forecast Category** field is based on the opportunity object, and one can rename the pick list as per business requirements.

Collaborative forecasting

Once you enable customizable forecasting, you will need to contact Salesforce to get it changed to collaborative. I am using a different instance now to walk you through the collaborative forecasting features. Most of the features are similar to customizable forecasting; the major difference we observe is that collaborative forecasting is not applicable when you have territory management in your instance or you have defined a custom fiscal year for your instance and you have no other option. If we have multicurrency enabled, then collaborative forecasting can be used. If the opportunity splits feature is used, collaborative forecasting will fit well. There is no **Submit** option as you will observe for collaborative forecasting, and also, the definitions of the forecast categories change in collaborative forecasting. It's no longer cumulative and the settings in the previous screenshot that we discussed will not apply here. Instead, it is just one-to-one mapping. A best case forecast will sum up only the opportunities in the best cases.

As shown in the following screenshot, for the first time, you will see the option to enable forecasting and set the default settings:

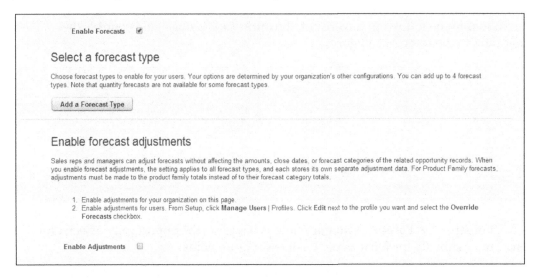

The same screen, once scrolled down, will have the option to select the defaults, as shown in the following screenshot:

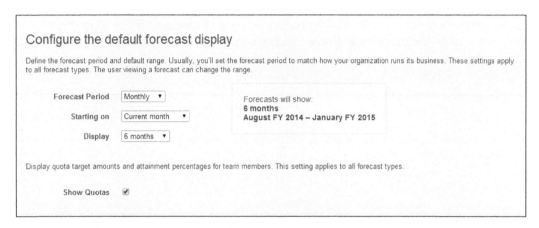

Add a forecast type (opportunity or product families), and then on the user record, you can enable the **Allow Forecasting** checkbox. This is shown in the following screenshot:

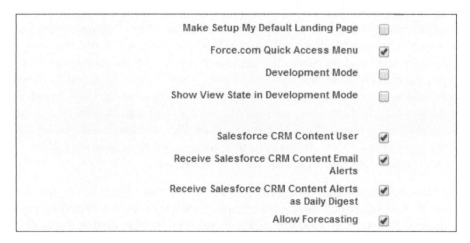

The sample UI is as shown in the following screenshot, which shows how a forecast looks once a user clicks on the **Forecasts** tab. The remainder of the configuration will be similar to what we discussed in the *Customizable forecasting* section. We won't be digging more here and readers are encouraged to get more information on this topic using the guide book from Salesforce available at `http://ap1.salesforce.com/help/pdfs/en/forecasts.pdf`.

The service cloud

The service cloud in Salesforce consists of modules that help to manage business processes that are required after a sales cycle has been completed and the company is providing support and service to the customers for the products that are sold. Salesforce provides modules such as case management, knowledge, entitlements, live agent, and so on, which can help customers raise requests, and agents can use these modules effectively to solve issues or customer requests. The service cloud has an excellent reporting utility like the report builder we discussed in *Chapter 3, Reports and Dashboards*, which can help to draw reports to measure the **Key Performance Indicators** (**KPIs**) for the call center industry.

The **case management** module primarily consists of the case object. There are features such as Email-to-Case, which can help a company manage the customer requests from e-mails directly. Consider an example of a call center or support center. Typically, we e-mail them or raise a case by phone, and we will be provided with a ticket number while a service representative works on it. In the sales cloud, our ticket number can be a case record and the case will be assigned to a representative who will be responsible for solving this case and providing a resolution.

Salesforce provides features such as case assignment and case escalation rules to automatically assign the case, and if a case is not solved automatically, it can be escalated to another representative or a manager. The case owner can be a queue or an individual. When the case owner is a queue, any of the representatives can pick the case from the queue and resolve it.

Salesforce provides a solutions object. One can enable the suggested solution feature that can autosuggest solutions to cases based on a built-in algorithm that automatically scores the relevancy of each solution to the particular case via word frequency, word proximity, case similarity, and related solutions.

The solutions module in Salesforce is a huge module, and it is recommended that you go to the **Support Settings** page and also to the solutions object to understand more. The following screenshot shows the support settings that can be configured. The navigation path is **Setup | Customize | Cases | Support Settings**.

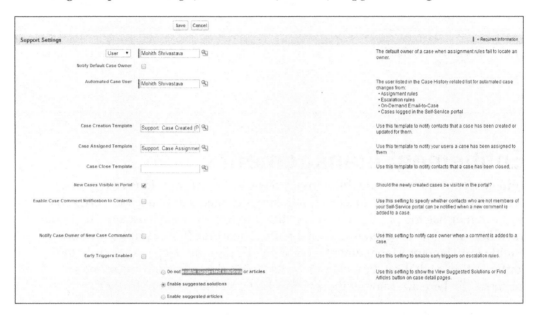

The solution settings can be used to enable the following features. The navigation path for the **Solution Settings** page is **Setup | Solutions | Solutions Settings**:

- **Enable Solution Browsing**
- **Enable Multilingual Solutions**
- **Enable HTML solutions** (this can't be disabled once enabled, so please be cautious)
- **Solution Summary**
- **Inline Solution Category Breadcrumbs**

The following screenshot shows the configuration screen:

Solution Settings

Specify the default settings for solutions.

Turn on the Browse Solutions section on the Solutions tab home page.
Enable Solution Browsing ☐

Turn on Multilingual Solutions.
Enable Multilingual Solutions ☐

Display the Language drop-down list on the Self-Service portal. The Language drop-down list allows Self-Service users to search solutions in the language of their choice or all languages in which solutions are supported.
Enable Multilingual Solution Search in Self-Service Portal ☐

Display the Language drop-down list on the public solutions page. The Language drop-down list allows users to search solutions in the language of their choice, or all languages in which solutions are supported.
Enable Multilingual Solution Search for Public Solutions ☐

Turn on HTML Solutions for your organization. WARNING: Once HTML Solutions is enabled, it cannot be disabled.
Enable HTML Solutions ☐

Display up to 150 characters of the solution in search results.
Solution Summary ☑

Display solution category breadcrumbs in search results.
Inline Solution Category Breadcrumbs ☑

Save | Cancel

Entitlement management

Your company may provide different levels of services for various customers. Before providing a service to a customer, support agents may need to verify that the customer has the provision and is entitled to the service. Please note that you must first navigate to settings and enable these features (for example, click on **Enable Entitlement Management**). We won't be digging deeper again into the configuration as that can be a chapter in itself and this is beyond the scope of this book. So here are some of the features that you may explore further:

- Milestones help agents to manage service levels in various stages of the entitlements. The basic navigation path to setting up entitlements is **Setup | Customize | Entitlement Management | Entitlements**.

- Service contracts can help agents to represent different kinds of customer support, such as warranties, subscriptions, or maintenance agreements. The navigation path is **Customize | Entitlement Management | Service Contracts**.

Salesforce.com provides three types of entitlement management options:

- **Entitlements Only**: In this process, service agents look at the account- or contact-related list to see whether the customer is eligible to receive the service. The entitlement object is configured and added as a related list to accounts and contacts.

- **Service Contracts with Entitlements**: In this process, a service contract object is configured and added as a related list to an account or a contact. Apart from agents looking into the entitlement-related list, they will also look into the service contract to figure out the level of service that needs to be provided. This may include a **Service Level Agreement (SLA)** agreed with the customer.

- **Service Contracts with Contract Line Items and Entitlements**: The navigation path to set up contract line items is **Customize | Entitlement Management | Service Contracts | Contract Line Items**. In this process, a service contract line item is configured and agents can provide a service based on entitlements and service contract line items.

Knowledge management

The business use case for using this module is as follows:

1. Your company has a self-service portal and you want to provide a set of content for your end users so that they can refer to it and solve their problem or know more about the products that the company offers.

2. You want to provide content for your sales or service representatives, which can help them in educating them about FAQs, solutions to known problems, and so on.

The greatest feature of knowledge management is the ability to search. Knowledge can be multilingual. One can set up an approval flow for knowledge. Knowledge in Salesforce follows a cycle from the draft state to the published state. The entire cycle can be managed to improve the quality of the content.

Articles are first drafted and then sent for review to article managers. Once reviewed, these are published. Articles can be versioned, and one can vote and rate them. Articles can be archived as well.

As an admin, it's important to note that in order to draft, publish, or archive, you will need a knowledge feature license.

There are two important concepts to understand about the knowledge module. They are as follows:

- **Article types**: Article types are containers. Each article type is an object in SFDC. You may have article types such as FAQs, marketing, and technology. You can have different layouts and templates for various article types.

- **Article data categories**: Article data categories help to categorize the article so that they can be easily searched. Based on data categories, the visibility of articles can also be set.

The navigation path for the knowledge management module is **App Setup | Knowledge**, as shown in the following screenshot:

One important thing that can help you in managing articles is navigating to the article management tab. This tab will only be visible if you are a knowledge user.

Content management

Content in Salesforce is an important feature to manage your files and documents securely. One can share content and also track the number of times the content is viewed and downloaded. A secure URL can be generated for sharing the content.

On navigating to **Setup | Content Deliveries | Settings**, one can configure content delivery options here.

The content delivery feature converts documents, such as Microsoft Word and PowerPoint files, into an online format that makes viewing content as easy as clicking on a link. You can send the content to recipients inside or outside your organization, and Salesforce.com tracks how frequently the content is viewed.

Live agent

This feature is like a live chat where a button is placed on the website or portal and on clicking it, the customer or end user can chat with the agent. As an administrator, you can route the chat based on the agent's skills.

Customer and partner community

The customer community is meant for collaboration between your customers and employees. Your contacts are end users and they become users of the system. Hence, you will see that contact records are also user records for the customer community.

The partner community is for collaboration between your partners and employees. Your partners may want to work and manage opportunities, leads, and contacts. There are special licenses available to manage these options.

Ideas and chatter answers

Ideas is a Salesforce standard feature where you can manage your ideas. Ideas have a voting mechanism where people can vote for an idea and leave comments.

The best example is the Salesforce idea website. Please feel free to post your ideas related to Salesforce features at `https://success.salesforce.com/ideaSearch`.

Chatter answers are similar to the self-service community where you can post questions and also answer them. People can like and comment on the answers or flag improper content. Based on the reputation earned by professionals who have answered and are active on the community, you can assign badges such as newbie, expert, and so on.

The best example for this is the success community, where you may want to post questions and get answers related to Salesforce administration and development. It is available at `https://success.salesforce.com/answers`.

The SFA maturity model

Salesforce is a complete matured tool for sales and service process management. You may have to write some business logic using workflows and triggers and approval processes along with the sales module of Salesforce.

The Salesforce sales module consists of the following:

- **Account management**: Account management in Salesforce is robust. The account object in Salesforce can be used for business-to-business or business-to-customer modules.

- **Contact management**: Salesforce provides a contact object to store contacts.

- **Lead management**: The lead conversion process of Salesforce provides a mechanism to convert leads into accounts, contacts, and opportunities.

- **Opportunity management**: Salesforce provides an opportunity object, and the stage field plays an important role in opportunity management.

- **Quote management**: Salesforce has quote items. You can use Salesforce to generate quotes, and these quotes can be mailed in a PDF format. The process from quote to cash can be complicated, and you will need a custom build using Apex triggers, Apex classes, and Visualforce on top of Salesforce. Companies such as Apptus have built sophisticated products around this.

- **Order management**: Although Salesforce has been late to pitch into this, with recent enhancements, the order object has been provided and accounts can have orders linked to them.

- **Forecasting**: Salesforce provides robust forecasting to predict the revenue.

- **Customer support**: The case management module with a service cloud console, knowledge module, and solutions module is strong enough to provide support to customers and also makes this CRM ideal to manage customer service and support.

- **Reporting**: Reporting in Salesforce is not so matured yet, and there are places for improvement. Products such as Tableau or QlikView have dominated the market, but using all these tools can be integrated with Salesforce to effectively report on Salesforce data.

- **ERP**: The ERP systems can be easily integrated with the Salesforce system through various APIs such as SOAP and REST, making the platform ideal.

One limitation of Salesforce is that huge data can create problems if your code and configuration are not properly architected.

Summary

This chapter summarized the sales and service cloud features provided by Salesforce.com. The Salesforce.com modules are huge in number, and it will take some time and some learning to get familiar with them. Salesforce.com has scope for administrators, developers, and functional consultants. The aim of this book is to get you started as an administrator on the Salesforce platform. This book is just the beginning of the vast learning of Salesforce.com. It's advisable that to get more practical insight, you should sign up for a free developer instance and play around with the configuration. You will soon find that the Salesforce platform is magic, and with just a few clicks, you can easily bring your users and business over to Salesforce.com.

Index

I

ideas
  about 133
  URL 133
ISNUMBER function 48

J

joined reports 61, 62

K

Key Performance Indicators (KPI) 128
knowledge management
  about 131, 132
  article data categories 132
  article types 131
  use case 131

L

license management
  about 5, 6
  featured license 7
  user license 7
license type
  Force.com App Subscription 7
  reference link 7
  Salesforce 6
  Salesforce Platform 7
line charts 64, 65
live agent 133
lookup relationship 27, 28

M

manual sharing 83, 86
many-to-many relationship 29, 30
master-detail relationship 29
matrix reports 60, 61
metric charts 69
mobile applications
  Salesforce 1 10
  Salesforce Classic 10
  Salesforce For Dashboards 10

O

objects, profile
  creating 13, 14
opportunity team 86, 87
Organization-Wide Defaults (OWD)
  about 77-81
  conclusions 79
  profile-level Modify All setting 82, 83
  profile-level View All setting 82, 83
  User Visibility settings 81
OWD settings
  Controlled By Parent 78
  Full Access 78
  Private 78
  Public Read 78
  Public Read Only 78
  Public Read/Write 78
  Public Read/Write/Transfer 78

P

page layouts 14, 42, 43
PARENTGROUPVAL
  about 58
  URL 58
partner community 133
password policy
  about 95
  settings, configuring 95, 96
pie charts 66
Platform as a Service (PaaS) 5, 117
PREVGROUPVAL 59, 60
profile
  configuring 15
  Salesforce console 16
profile-level Modify All setting 82, 83
profile-level View All setting 82, 83
profile management
  about 12
  applications 14
  fields 13, 14
  objects 13, 14
  page layouts 14
  tabs 14

R

S

T

Thank you for buying

Salesforce Essentials for Administrators

About Packt Publishing

Packt, pronounced 'packed', published its first book "Mastering phpMyAdmin for Effective MySQL Management" in April 2004 and subsequently continued to specialize in publishing highly focused books on specific technologies and solutions.

Our books and publications share the experiences of your fellow IT professionals in adapting and customizing today's systems, applications, and frameworks. Our solution based books give you the knowledge and power to customize the software and technologies you're using to get the job done. Packt books are more specific and less general than the IT books you have seen in the past. Our unique business model allows us to bring you more focused information, giving you more of what you need to know, and less of what you don't.

Packt is a modern, yet unique publishing company, which focuses on producing quality, cutting-edge books for communities of developers, administrators, and newbies alike. For more information, please visit our website: www.packtpub.com.

About Packt Enterprise

In 2010, Packt launched two new brands, Packt Enterprise and Packt Open Source, in order to continue its focus on specialization. This book is part of the Packt Enterprise brand, home to books published on enterprise software – software created by major vendors, including (but not limited to) IBM, Microsoft, and Oracle, often for use in other corporations. Its titles will offer information relevant to a range of users of this software, including administrators, developers, architects, and end users.

Writing for Packt

We welcome all inquiries from people who are interested in authoring. Book proposals should be sent to author@packtpub.com. If your book idea is still at an early stage and you would like to discuss it first before writing a formal book proposal, contact us; one of our commissioning editors will get in touch with you.

We're not just looking for published authors; if you have strong technical skills but no writing experience, our experienced editors can help you develop a writing career, or simply get some additional reward for your expertise.

Salesforce.com
Customization Handbook

Customize Salesforce to automate your business requirements

Rakesh Gupta   Sagar Pareek   [PACKT] enterprise

Salesforce.com Customization Handbook

ISBN: 978-1-84968-598-6   Paperback: 454 pages

Customize Salesforce to automate your business requirements

1. Learn the concepts of Salesforce.com to automate business processes.

2. Streamline your sales process and improve collaboration in your organization.

3. A step-by-step approach to online course design to make your business more reliable and productive.

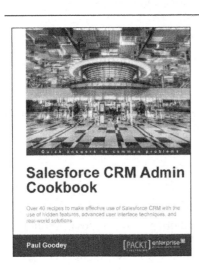

Salesforce CRM Admin
Cookbook

Over 40 recipes to make effective use of Salesforce CRM with the use of hidden features, advanced user interface techniques, and real-world solutions

Paul Goodey   [PACKT] enterprise

Salesforce CRM Admin Cookbook

ISBN: 978-1-84968-424-8   Paperback: 266 pages

Over 40 recipes to make effective use of Salesforce CRM with the use of hidden features, advanced user interface techniques, and real-world solutions

1. Implement advanced user interface techniques to improve the look and feel of Salesforce CRM.

2. Discover hidden features and hacks that extend the standard configuration to provide enhanced functionality and customization.

3. Build real-world process automation, using the detailed recipes to harness the full power of Salesforce CRM.

Please check **www.PacktPub.com** for information on our titles

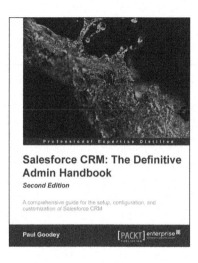

Salesforce CRM: The Definitive Admin Handbook

Second Edition

ISBN: 978-1-78217-052-5   Paperback: 426 pages

A comprehensive guide for the setup, configuration, and customization of Salesforce CRM

1. Updated for Spring '13, this book covers best practice administration principles, real-world experience, and critical design considerations for setting up and customizing Salesforce CRM.

2. Analyze data within Salesforce by using reports, dashboards, custom reports, and report builder.

3. A step-by-step guide offering clear guidance for the customization and administration of the Salesforce CRM application.

Developing Applications with Salesforce Chatter

ISBN: 978-1-78217-116-4   Paperback: 130 pages

Leverage the power of Chatter to boost collaboration in your organization

1. Understand Salesforce Chatter and its architecture.

2. Configure and set up Chatter for your organization.

3. Improve Chatter features by utilizing Apex and Visualforce Pages.

Please check **www.PacktPub.com** for information on our titles